THE CONTENT MARKETING EQUATION

Start or Grow Your Online Business Using the Power of Blogging, Podcasting, and Content Creation

Praise for
The Content Marketing Equation

What's uniquely valuable about *The Content Marketing Equation* is that Anthony provides details—both from his own experience, and from researched case studies—that you can immediately implement in your own business or content marketing strategy. This isn't a vague "why you should become a better marketer" book, instead, Anthony gives us the nuts and bolts and how to get it done.

— Dan Andrews,
Host of The Tropical MBA Podcast

Having spent the better part of the decade living and breathing content at BuzzFeed, I have to say this is a great roadmap on how to activate in the Social World. Anthony does a tremendous job at simplifying the subject and most importantly making it actionable. He gives super clear steps, uses real world anecdotal examples to paint the picture, and includes a ton of resources where the reader can apply his principals immediately. It's a great read for anyone thinking about getting into content creation and brand building.

— Stephen Loguidice,
Senior Vice President of Global Brand Development
at BuzzFeed

Anthony's guidance significantly increased my first business's impact and revenue. If you choose to implement his strategy, you will increase your authority, efficiency, and profitability. Bottom line: read this book multiple times.

— Alex Barker,
Coach for high performers, Speaker, Author & Coffee Lover

Content marketing is a subject about which many people have misconceptions. In his book, Anthony outlines the truth about pursuing a content brand. He emphasizes something that many other resources overlook: revenue. This is great because without revenue, you won't be a content marketer for long! Great read for those interested in developing a brand from scratch on the web where content abounds but great content is still a great opportunity.

— **Anna Wickman,**
Content Specialist,
AnnaWickham.com

No doubt, this book is going to change the face of marketing and commerce on the Internet. Content marketing is the future and the strategy Anthony outlines is easy to execute and wildly effective. If you're a small business owner struggling to "crack" the online world, then this is a must read!

— **Josh Stanton,**
Co-Founder of Screw the Nine to Five Lifestyle Business

THE CONTENT MARKETING EQUATION

Start or Grow Your Online Business Using the Power of Blogging, Podcasting, and Content Creation

ANTHONY FASANO

The Content Marketing Equation:
Start or Grow Your Online Business Using the Power of Blogging,
Podcasting, and Content Creation

Published by American Consumer News, LLC.
First edition: February 2017
ISBN: 978-1541333246

Cover Design: Rebecca McKeever
Editing: Craft Your Content
Book Design: James Woosley (FreeAgentPress.com)
Printing: Amazon CreateSpace

TABLE OF CONTENTS

Chapter 5: Capture [C3] – Capture Information 87

Chapter 6: Monetization – The Scary M Word 111

Chapter 7: Conclusion – It's Time for You to Take Action 133

List of Case Studies, which are included throughout the book

FOREWORD

by Matthew Paulson

In 2006, I was a broke college student with limited job opportunities and a dream of making money on the Internet. At the time, there were no trustworthy Internet business experts to follow, and there were no proven paths to make money online. I had to build my online business the hard way, by trying a whole lot of business ideas and making a lot of mistakes. It took me a full five years of experimenting and trying different online business models before I identified one that worked.

That model, now known as the Authority Publishing Model, involves selecting a profitable niche in which you have expertise, creating valuable content, building an email list, and selling products and services to your audience. The Authority Publishing Model is simple, straightforward, and it actually works.

I launched my current business, MarketBeat, using the Authority Publishing Model in 2011. The mission of MarketBeat is to make real-time stock research information available to investors at all levels. We do this through our website and our daily investment newsletter, which has grown to have more than 450,000 subscribers. By identifying a profitable niche, creating great content for the people in our niche, and publishing that content through the right channels, our business has been able to achieve massive results in a relatively short period of time. MarketBeat is on track to generate $3 million in revenue in 2016, and was recently recognized by *Inc. Magazine* as one of the 5,000 fastest-growing privately-held companies in the United States. I don't tell you all of these big numbers to brag, but rather to illustrate the kind of success the Authority Publishing Model (and years of hard work!) can lead to.

When I was getting started, there were no good available resources that taught the Authority Publishing Model. I stumbled my way through building my online business, and made a lot of mistakes along the way—but you don't have to do that. My good friend, Anthony Fasano, has put together a step-by-step guide that teaches you exactly how to build your own content-driven authority publishing business in his new book, *The Content Marketing Equation*.

The equation, **NVC³**, teaches **niche** selection, how to create **valuable** content, how to publish content through the right **channels,** how to publish content **consistently**, how to **capture** information while building an email list, and how to actually **make money** online. *The Content Marketing Equation* is the one book I wish I'd had when I was first trying to build an online business, in 2006.

There are a lot of resources that teach how to build online businesses, including my book *40 Rules for Internet Business Success*, but many of them are written by people who have never actually built an online business, or who have only ever made money online by teaching other people to make money online. Rest assured, Anthony Fasano is not another of this type of internet marketing guru.

I first met Anthony a few years back at a conference for location-independent entrepreneurs in Austin, TX. At the time, he was working on getting his engineering coaching business off the ground. I figured he would be the next in a long line of part-time entrepreneurs who have a moderate level of success, but I underestimated him.

Since I first met Anthony, he's built profitable online businesses in many different niches. He launched a successful website and podcast for engineers called *The Engineering Career Coach Podcast*. He has revitalized the New York State Society of Professional Engineers through video marketing and published a book titled *Engineer Your Own Success,* that teaches engineers to advance in their careers. He struck a deal with National Italian American Foundation and launched *The Italian American Podcast* to their audience. He even produces and built up an audience for an online radio show called *The Stem Cell Podcast,* which he doesn't even host himself!

You probably won't see Anthony headlining a major digital marketing conference or plastering his name all over the Internet, because he's not worried about becoming famous—and he's too busy building his own online businesses.

While he comes across as modest and unassuming, don't let that fool you. Anthony is the real deal. He easily makes six figures in revenue from his online businesses, and he is a talented entrepreneur from whom we can all learn something. If you have an existing business or are considering launching your own online business, I strongly recommend that you read and closely follow the formula outlined in *The Content Marketing Equation.*

Matthew Paulson
November 1ˢᵗ, 2016

INTRODUCTION

by Anthony Fasano

How to Use this Book to Grow Your Business with my Content Marketing Equation (NVC³)

One day in 2008, I was sitting in a cubicle, working as a civil engineer, when it hit me. There are too many opportunities available today for Internet entrepreneurship for me to be stuck inside of a cubicle for 50 hours a week.

I immediately started learning everything I could about online marketing and how to grow a reputation and a business. Fast-forward to 2016, and my life is totally different.

I now work from home, am married with three children, and just finished a 42-day trip through Italy where I connected with family that I found a year ago through online research.

In the pages that follow, I will share with you the equation that I have used to achieve success over the past eight years. Since that epiphany in 2008, I have:

- Written and self-published a book for engineers on professional development, which was picked up by a major publisher because of its impressive sales.

- Traveled to over 25 U.S. States, from Maine to Alaska, speaking to and sharing my book's insights with engineers.

- Built the number-one career development website for engineers, called *The Engineering Career Coach*.

- Created two extremely popular podcasts for engineers, that cumulatively have been downloaded over 1.5 million times in the last three years.

- Raised $13,000 online for a project where my eight-year-old daughter and I wrote and published two children's books, which we delivered to pediatric cancer centers across the United States.

- Helped to build the first podcast in the stem cell industry. It is an extremely popular show, and has generated an income of over $100,000 in a 12-month period.

- Started the first podcast on Italian-American heritage, which involved interviewing celebrities including Adriana Trigiani, Lidia Bastianich, Tony Reali, and Mike Piazza.

- Been hired as the Executive Director at a non-profit association for engineers in New York where, using my online skills, I helped the organization achieve its first membership increase in seven years, while revamping their online presence to include videos, which have become very popular.

I could go on, but I think you get the idea. The ability to leverage the Internet to grow projects and businesses has changed my life for the better. Because of this, small business owners and entrepreneurs looking to build or start businesses online often ask me how I "did it." This recurring question has made me take a hard look at the core strategies I used, so I would be able to adequately explain them.

Due to my engineering education and experience. I am a very analytical thinker. I am always looking at things in a black and white, linear way, and trying to optimize them. Looking at the businesses I had been involved with, I realised there was a pattern or an equation that I had used to grow each one. The common thread was content development, but there was also a specific process.

Upon realizing this, I took the time to sketch out the equation, and it looked like this:

The Content Marketing Equation = NVC³

- N is for Niche – Select a Niche
- V is for Value – Create Valuable Content
- C1 is for Channels – Publish Content through the Right Channels
- C2 is for Consistency – Publish Content Consistently
- C3 is for Capture – Capture Information

After looking at the available advice on content marketing, I became sick of online marketing gurus talking about all the money they made, but never really explaining how. So I decided to write this book, which will walk entrepreneurs through very specific practices that they can utilize to grow their online businesses through content development. The process encapsulated in NVC³ also applies to non-profit associations, and really any organization that wants to leverage the power of the Internet in order to grow.

Not only does this book walk you through the equation step-by-step, but—at the end of each chapter—it provides case studies that show how I have successfully used this formula again and again. I want you to see that this equation is real and it works. All the case studies in this book are from my own experience.

I have also included exercises at the end of each chapter, so you can apply the steps of my equation to your business immediately. In fact, I recommend that as you read the book, you do the exercises at the end of each chapter before you proceed to the next. This will allow you to maximize the effects of the equation in your endeavors.

It's time to supercharge the growth of your business with The Content Marketing Equation.

CHAPTER 1

Niche [N] –
Select a Niche

1. You must have a niche in content marketing.

A niche is defined as a distinct segment of the market.

Trying to create content without focusing on a specific niche is like trying to open a restaurant that serves every kind of food—American, Italian, Chinese, Polish...

What would happen if you tried to open a restaurant like this? You probably would not succeed. You would have to purchase and carry different inventory for each nationality. Not only would carrying all this inventory be expensive, but you also would need a lot of physical space to store it, which would also be costly. You would be fighting an uphill battle.

This is what most content marketers do.

In my experience, nine out of ten content marketers create content for an audience that is too broad. Most of them fall into the very dangerous trap of thinking that the more people they create content for, the more prospective customers they'll have access to, and therefore the more customers they'll have. What actually happens is the opposite.

When you are serving too broad a market, the content isn't very interesting to many people, which makes it hard to gain traction and build a following. Content is free and plentiful these days, and so to win at content marketing you need to create very specific content that will be remarkably interesting to a particular audience.

Think back to the example of opening a restaurant. In addition to inventory woes, if you try to open a restaurant that serves many different national styles of food, you won't be seen as an expert in any one type. However, if you focused on one style of cuisine, like Italian, you could become the best Italian restaurant in your area, and attract more customers looking for excellent Italian food. Italian cuisine lovers from all over could hear about your reputation and flock to your restaurant.

Think about the products and/or services you offer,

or you plan to offer, with your business. Now, think about how many customers you would need for your business to be successful, based on your sale prices. It's not that many customers, is it?

Most business owners can have a successful business with hundreds of customers or less, yet they try to create content for a market segment with millions.

When we started *The Stem Cell Podcast*, we originally planned to focus on information that would be interesting to both stem cell scientists *and* lay people wanting to learn about stem cells. We quickly realized that the content wouldn't be as powerful or interesting to either of those market segments if we went down that route.

So we decided to focus on the stem cell scientists, and made our show a detailed exploration of current research in the stem cell field. Doing this enabled us to become the go-to podcast for stem cell scientists, which in turn allowed us to generate podcast sponsorships in excess of $100,000 per year. Needless to say, sponsorship mostly came from companies looking to sell products to stem cell scientists.

The rest of this chapter will walk you through the steps you can take to select a niche for your business, with examples from my own experience. Make sure you spend the time you need to select the right niche for your business, as it really does mean everything.

Though it may seem counterintuitive, this also applies if you are already a business owner, as you may need to narrow down your niche and offerings, in order to increase your market traction and revenue.

Let's get started on selecting your niche.

2. Start with your expertise.

Selecting a niche prior to starting a content-driven business, or narrowing down your niche if you already own a business, is extremely important. But how exactly do you find the right niche?

The first step is to consider a niche you already have expertise in. While this is not mandatory, there are many benefits to selecting a niche with which you are already familiar.

To start, you will be able to relate to others in this niche, since you have experienced what it is like to work in the field. This makes it much easier to create content for these individuals, because you know what they deal with on a day-to-day basis.

When I was working as an engineer, I knew that I wanted to provide career coaching and guidance to engineers, because I knew the challenges they encounter in trying to develop their careers. Most of these challenges can be overcome by developing better interpersonal skills.

However, I fell into the dangerous trap that catches out most content marketers.

After attending a very costly executive coaching school, I figured I could coach anybody in any field on any topic. Why limit myself (and my income) to engineers? Consequently,

I started my first business, *Powerful Purpose Associates*, and began creating a ton of content, for everyone. I wrote weekly blog posts, weekly newsletters called the Monday Morning Motivator, and even a daily email known as A Daily Boost from Your Professional Partner. Though I was creating this content based on my experience as an engineer, I was doing so in a way that attempted to make it benefit virtually anyone. Thus, it was very general in nature, and not actually targeted to any one niche.

I ended up inspiring a lot people with my content, but never had enough traction with any one segment to build a profitable business. Then one day it hit me. I realized that most of my content was specific to the challenges I had faced as a developing engineer. I immediately stopped creating content in a voice aimed at everyone, I renamed my business *The Engineering Career Coach*, and changed the main company URL from PowerfulPurpose.com to EngineeringCareerCoach.com. Only after that was I able to build my first successful content-based business.

My content went from inspirational to actionable, because I could specifically help engineers develop professionally, based on my own experience.

The other major benefit of this route is that your experience in a specific field allows you to really position yourself as an expert. In my case, I had obtained my professional engineering license at the very young age of 23, and also achieved a very high level of 'Associate' in the engineering firm that I worked for at age 27. These accomplishments gave me credibility as someone who knew how to advance in an engineering career, and made me the perfect person to build The Engineering Career Coach brand.

Between my ability to understand what my prospective readers were going through and my expertise in the field, I was able to create content with extremely practical advice for engineers who wanted to follow it. As niched down as The Engineering Career Coach website is, we niched it down even further with a second podcast, which I will talk about in the case study section at the end of this chapter.

I don't think it is *an absolute must* to have experience in the field that you plan to build a content-based brand in, but it is extremely helpful. There are people like Pat Flynn, who was laid off in his position as an architect and ended up building a massive following through a website he built called SmartPassiveIncome.com. Flynn generates over $100,000 per month now through his website. However, he started by building a website that was focused on a niche that was all about helping people pass the LEED AP (Leadership in Energy and Environmental Design Accredited Professional), architecturally-focused exam. Flynn had passed the exam in his prior position, and wanted to use his expertise to help others do the same. Flynn's *Smart Passive Income* website is a gold mine for content creators, and I highly recommend subscribing to his content.

When selecting your niche, start narrow with your expertise, as you can potentially widen it later. You're better off being an expert in one field, with very specific content, than a jack-of-all-trades and master of none.

3. Do your market research on your desired niches.

Another important part of selecting the niche you should serve is researching some of the statistics of the different market segments you're looking at.

Just because you have expertise in a field doesn't mean your niche can provide enough revenue to build a sustainable business.

The following are some data points you should consider when deciding whether or not your niche is suitable for building a revenue-generating business.

Size of the niche.

Size doesn't always matter. You can build a massive revenue-generating content creation business off a niche that is very small in size, as long as its prospective consumers will spend enough money for access.

To estimate the potential size of niche, consider using tools like the Google Keyword Planner and Google Trends, both of which will give you insight into how many people are doing searches associated with your niche.

There are many websites and articles that can help you determine the size of your target market. Here are a few:

- The U.S. Small Business Administration site:
  - https://www.sba.gov/starting-business/
    how-start-business/understand-your-market
- You can consult the website Quora—here is one example on niche size:
  - https://www.quora.com/
    How-does-one-estimate-the-size-of-a-niche-market#
- Tim Ferriss wrote a good article that touches on niche size:
  - http://fourhourworkweek.com/2011/09/24/how-
    to-create-a-million-dollar-business-this-weekend-
    examples-appsumo-mint-chihuahuas

Age demographics and revenue per person.

You should attempt to determine the age and revenue of people in your niche. GSood estimates of this information are available through relatively quick online research. One of the best tools I have found is the United States Census Bureau website, namely their fact tables, which you can find here: https://www.census.gov/quickfacts/
table/PST045215/00

Future industry growth trends.

Of course, you should also consider fast-growing or emerging markets when selecting a niche for your business. There are tons of resources and articles online that can help you identify these markets. Here are two really helpful articles I have found, which are relevant at the time of the publication of this book:

- Pew Research Center:

- http://www.pewresearch.org/fact-tank/2016/03/31/10-demographic-trends-that-are-shaping-the-u-s-and-the-world
- NicheHacks:
  - http://nichehacks.com/category/niche-market-ideas

The more time you spend on research, and the more detailed information you obtain, the easier it will be to decide on the most profitable niche. Just don't get stuck in a 'paralysis by analysis' situation, where you end up spending so much time researching that you lose valuable business building time.

4. Investigate URLs and naming options.

At this point, you have decided on a niche, and confirmed that the niche is a viable one, based on market research. Now, you need to think about naming your brand.

The name and URL for your business is more important than you think. In a world of information overload, people must be able to understand what you offer and if you can help them, in a matter of seconds.

My rule of thumb is: when you tell someone the name of your company or they land on your website, they should immediately know whether or not your site is for them.

I know some people may argue with me on this point, and say that they want to go with a catchy or eye-pleasing name, but typically brands that pull that off have a ton of marketing money to spend. Most content marketers don't.

As I mentioned earlier, my first business was called Powerful Purpose Associates. It's an interesting name, but doesn't tell you who the company serves, or how it serves them. For a counter example, The Engineering Career Coach makes it pretty clear what the mission of the company is.

The name of your business is super-critical to its success, mainly because people today have very short attention spans. If you can't make it clear that you can help them, they will have moved on to the next source of information in seconds. In my experience, you have less than 10 seconds to engage someone when they land on your website, and its name will contribute to your success in engaging these visitors.

The actual URL of the website may be just as important, if not more important, than the actual company name. The main reason for this is that search engines like Google put a lot of weight on the actual search terms in the URL of the page. Before settling on The Engineering Career Coach as a company name, I made sure that EngineeringCareerCoach.com was available.

Think about it. If someone is doing a web search for engineering career coaching, engineering career guidance, or engineering career questions, Google is going to rank my website pretty high up for those terms because my URL tells them that this is the kind of information I have on my site. Does PowerfulPurpose.com tell Google that? No, it doesn't.

Let me be clear that this is not a book on search engine optimization (SEO), and I will not cover the specifics of SEO, because they are likely to change often. However, having search terms in your URL is always a good thing. Consider reading up on SEO if you plan to create content, a subject that I will discuss more in another section. (For clarification, SEO is defined by Wikipedia as "the process of affecting the visibility of a website or a web page in a search engine's unpaid results—often referred to as "natural," "organic," or "earned" results.")

My recommendation is that if you are just starting a new business and plan on creating content, don't use your own name as the name and URL of the business. This puts you at a severe disadvantage compared to those in your niche who have named their businesses strategically. You can still attach your name to the business or website in some way, like The Engineering Career Coach with Anthony Fasano.

Not only is this important while establishing your business, it could also play a key role in selling your business in the future. Selling a website with your name on it, built on your personal brand, will be more difficult than selling a strategically-named business.

5. Look for partnering organizations and other low-cost marketing channels.

Another important consideration when selecting your niche is marketing—specifically any low-cost marketing channels that might be available in a particular niche.

I am a co-owner of a podcast entitled *The Stem Cell Podcast*, and my partners and I utilized this strategy to massively grow our listener base. We contacted a local non-profit association that served stem cell scientists, and we asked them if we could develop a partnership with them. They were looking for content for their members, and we were looking for exposure.

We signed a two-year agreement that made them an official sponsor of the podcast, and in return they shared our podcast through all their online avenues, including their website and monthly newsletter. Think about the power of this for our podcast and brand. We were a relatively new show, and after this agreement, our episodes were emailed out to a targeted list of thousands of stem cell scientists, at no cost to us. That's right, the agreement was a partnership with no exchange of money.

In addition to them sharing our content online, they also gave us a booth in the main area at their annual conference in Stockholm, Sweden. About 5,000 stem cell scientists attended this conference. We received the booth and free admission to the conference, on the condition that we conducted podcast interviews while there and published an episode around the interviews. This opportunity gave us a lot of great exposure and, of course, a trip to Sweden, which we thoroughly enjoyed.

You may be thinking, how did this partnership *really* help us as an online business, if we didn't make any money off it directly? The partnership provided free marketing to our very specific audience, which we may have otherwise struggled to reach, and we turned that marketing investment into revenue, through other sponsorships.

The relationship also gave us credibility, and made it easier for us to close paying sponsorships because we had an affiliation with the field's most authoritative association. Thus, the sponsors knew we would be securing publicity for them through the association's channels. As an example, we met a company at that conference who ended up becoming a long-term sponsor.

This is not the only podcast that I have taken this approach with. I received a press pass for my podcast entitled The Civil Engineering Podcast that allowed me to attend a large civil engineering conference. I was not charged a fee to attend, and I was able to interview attendees in order to create a conference summary episode. In return, the association shared the episode with their membership, which consists of approximately 150,000 members, all of whom are in my podcast's specific niche. You can see this very successful piece of content here: http://engineeringcareercoach.com/asce

I have a similar arrangement with a podcast entitled *The Italian American Podcast,* which is featured on a major non-profit association's website in return for the non-profit being an official sponsor of the podcast. No money changes hands: the non-profit's credibility is transformed into increased traffic for *The Italian American Podcast*, which translates into revenue from companies who pay to promote themselves on our platform. I will tell you more about this partnership, and how we have gained some celebrity interviews from it, in the case study section at the end of this chapter.

Considering possible low-cost marketing avenues when you select your niche can be critical to the pace of your brand's growth. In my different businesses, free marketing techniques (as described above) have catapulted my content to being the most read and downloaded resources in their respective niches.

These partnerships are so important because most content marketers are self-funded, which is a nice way to say they have no money and no investors. Therefore, rapid growth through a partnership may be the quickest way to generate income.

6. Understand the competition.

In any business—whether it is content-based or not—understanding the competition is crucial. It is very difficult, but not impossible, to gain market share from businesses that are already established in a niche. If you want to learn more about positioning yourself in an industry, consider reading *Positioning: The Battle for your Mind* by Al Ries and Jack Trout. The book is an oldie but goodie with a lot of timeless advice, and was updated in 2001.

If there are other businesses in the niche you are considering, that doesn't mean you should abandon your desire to start yours. Consider the age and market penetration of those businesses by asking the following questions:

- **If they are content-based businesses, what level of quality content is the competition publishing?**
  Look to see if their content is well-written and optimized for search, or just words put up on a page because they needed to publish content. If their content isn't well-written or produced, they most likely don't have a lot of traction.

- **Are they publishing across multiple channels like a blog, videos, and a podcast?**
  I had written hundreds of articles on The Engineering Career Coach website, and then I decided to start The Engineering Career Coach podcast, which added a completely different dimension to the site. Many people told me that engineers would never listen to the podcast, yet today the podcast has been downloaded over one million times. This gave us access to engineers through a completely different channel, one that competitors didn't think was valuable. I will dive into this topic in more detail later in the book. You have to consider whether it might be possible to penetrate the market faster through channels that your competitors aren't using yet.

- **What kind of market penetration do the other businesses have?**
  It is hard to surpass a business or content site that is well established and popular, so you must do your best to gauge the traction these competitors have. As a first step, take a look at their social media sites. Are they active? How

many followers do they have? While businesses tend to inflate their social media channels by purchasing followers, a thorough look can still give you an idea of their popularity. This is especially true for the nature of the interactions with followers on their posts.

Another thing to look at is the Amazon.com reviews for the company's products, or any books that the site authors may have written. If they have a podcast, how many iTunes ratings and reviews do they have? This data alone will give you a clear picture of how much traction their website really has.

By running through these questions, you should be able to get a good feel for how successful a business is in a matter of minutes.

On most of our content sites, we were first to market, which is why we used the word THE in front of our podcasts. For example, *The Italian American Podcast*, *The Stem Cell Podcast*, *The Civil Engineering Podcast*, and *The Engineering Career Coach Podcast*. If you get to market first, consider placing "The" in front of the name as a way to cement your brand as the industry leader. Then it will be difficult for new competitors to surpass *you*.

Don't worry, the coming chapters will give you a proven blueprint for building that audience.

7. Consider all potential sources of revenue.

Failing to consider all potential sources of revenue is where I messed up with The Engineering Career Coach brand and website, and I will explain how you can avoid making the same mistake.

Most content marketers start a website out of passion for a specific topic. They write amazing articles that start to get a ton of traffic. Then they realize their followers want more content. Unfortunately, the time it takes to prepare more quality content really adds up, and—all of a sudden—they are creating content on a crazy schedule, but earning absolutely no money for it. This is what is commonly referred to as a hamster wheel.

In this content hamster wheel, if you stop creating content, your traffic will slow down, and your site will start to die off. Yet if you continue, you will be stuck working like crazy, essentially on a treadmill to nowhere. Unless, of course, you have some plans for monetizing the site. We will cover monetization in more detail towards the end of the book; however, at this point, I do want to discuss it from a big picture perspective.

I don't expect you to have all of your revenue sources planned out from day one. In fact, in most cases, you can't. As a content brand grows, different opportunities arise, and you can consider these as they come. Still, from day one, you should brainstorm and come up with at least five potential sources of revenue.

Here is a list of some basic potential revenue sources (note that the list may change based on your niche):

- Google AdSense (Google will insert niche-specific ads onto your site, in locations you specify, and they will pay you every time someone clicks on them),

- Private Banner Ads that you can sell directly to companies targeting your niche,

- Podcast sponsorships that you (or a third party that you retain, like Midroll.com) can sell to companies targeting your niche,

- YouTube Ads on your videos,

- Your own products and services, which may include books, coaching, speaking, events, and more,

- Donations from your followers using PayPal or websites like Patreon, which allows your audience to make donations for the free content you are creating.

When I started The Engineering Career Coach website, I never gave much thought to the revenue side of things. I basically thought I would build up a lot of great content for younger, developing engineers, and they would pay me for career coaching. That was my plan. My plan didn't work.

What I failed to consider were two key points:

1. Younger engineers don't have a lot of disposable income to spend on career and personal development.

2. Most engineers don't know what career coaching is, and how it can help them.

Based on these points, The Engineering Career Coach website earned very little money for a very long time. I was on the hamster wheel for a while.

At this point, the site does okay with revenue, generating just over six figures, but our profit margin is still fairly low, which is something we are working on improving to this day. To get our revenue up, we started an online coaching community for engineers at a low price point, we have added some sizeable podcast sponsors, and we have started running events for associations. We are, however, considering selling the site to a company that has more products and services to sell directly to engineers.

If I started over and thought out more revenue sources, I might have found my way to podcasting a few years earlier, or started doing content development for associations earlier on.

Bottomline: Create a revenue plan *before* you start developing your content, even if it changes along the way.

8. CASE STUDIES on Niche Selection

I want ensure this book is practical and actionable for you; therefore, at the end of each chapter, I will provide one or a few case studies, based on the chapter's topic. These case studies are mostly examples from my personal experience building multiple six-figure online content businesses.

Case Study #1 – The Civil Engineering Podcast

In Section 2 of this chapter I talked about selecting a niche based on your own career expertise. Doing this led me to create The Engineering Career Coach brand. However, there are hundreds of different types of engineers, across the world. My area of expertise was civil engineering.

Civil engineering is one of the largest engineering disciplines in the world. A few years into developing the site, I started to feel that 'engineering' was too broad a niche. The solution I landed on was to focus in even more and make the site about 'civil engineering.'

I considered how to do this for a while, and did some research into the type of engineering disciplines represented by those who had subscribed to our mailing list. I kept the main brand as The Engineering Career Coach, but I added a second podcast called *The Civil Engineering Podcast*, which allowed me to engage directly with civil engineers, and also create another revenue channel for podcast sponsors.

Another important aspect to this decision was the fact that right around this time, I took on a partner in the company, and he took over half of the content creation, thereby slightly slowing the hamster wheel for me.

Case Study #2 – The National Italian American Foundation

Low-cost marketing channels was the subject of Section 5 in this chapter. This subject came up for me a few years ago, when I attended a great conference for podcasters called Podcast Movement. It was at this conference, while sitting in the audience, that the idea for *The Italian American Podcast* came to me.

One year later, the podcast was twenty episodes in and doing great. As I mentioned, we were able to create a partnership with The National Italian American Foundation (NIAF) where they became the official sponsor of the podcast.

Creating this partnership was relatively easy. A cousin of mine told me about NIAF. I investigated the organization, and then became a member. Soon after, my co-host and I contacted the NIAF President, with whom we scheduled a meeting. In the meeting, we explained to him how our mission was similar to theirs; however, we were using a media channel they hadn't used yet, so it would make sense for us to team up. A few months later we had a formal partnership agreement in place, and both organizations have benefitted greatly from the partnership thus far.

As part of the partnership agreement, they share our content with all of their members and followers, and we have free access to their two big galas each year, where we can conduct interviews. NIAF's following is pretty big, with over 100,000 Facebook fans and 100,000 email subscribers, so this partnership has really helped us to grow our listener base.

We also had the opportunity to interview Major League Baseball hall of fame player Mike Piazza, in April before his July induction, but released the interview right around the ceremony. This was all possible because we found this low-cost avenue for marketing our podcast and gaining access to big-name guests.

9. Your turn to take action on niche selection.

Now it's your turn to take action on your niche development, marketing, and revenue projections.

NICHE SELECTION

On the lines below, brainstorm at least five possible niches that you can serve through content creation. Even if a few seem like a stretch, it's better to start with more and weed out the weaker ones along the way.

I strongly urge you to take action and complete this exercise now—your success in building a successful content-marketing business depends on taking real steps, however small, towards your goal. If you already have a business, then use these exercises to confirm that your niche is defined well enough—could it be niched down further?

_____

_____

_____

_____

_____

_____

Now, using the parameters in Sections 3 and 5 of this chapter, circle one or two niches that make the most sense for you and your business. It would be ideal to get to one, but if two are attractive then select both, and the next exercise will help you narrow them down further.

MARKETING AVENUES

Now, using the information in Section 6 of this chapter, find possible partnerships that you can create in the niche(s) you selected. Consider non-profit associations that have access to your niche, but don't have the quality or quantity of content that you can provide. List all of the possibilities for your niche(s). Again, take the real-world step of generating ideas, and you're a little bit closer to achieving success.

_____

_____

_____

_____

_____

_____

REVENUE SOURCES

On the lines below, list all possible sources of revenue for your selected niche(s). See Section 7 of this chapter for various revenue ideas. Doing this exercise today is a truly productive task, that will ultimately lead to your future income.

_____

_____

_____

_____

_____

_____

Once you have completed these exercises, review your original niche selections and decide on which is the best for your content-creation business.

Now you have a well-defined niche for your business, with some low-cost marketing avenues in mind and some projected revenue sources. In the next chapter, I'll give you strategies for developing highly valuable content for your selected niche.

CHAPTER 2

Value [V] –
Create Valuable Content

1. Review existing industry content. Can you improve it?

Now that you've nailed down your niche, you'll need to start creating content for your market. In this chapter, I will give you several strategies for determining topics of interest for your target market.

Before we dive into those strategies, I recommend your first step be to review existing industry content. If you followed along with Chapter 1, you have probably already identified the top competitors in your niche.

It's time to revisit their websites and take a closer look at their content. Subscribe to their newsletters and social media sites, so you can continue to see their content as they publish it.

Consume their content in whatever form they publish it—blogs, videos, podcasts, etc. Think about how you can create better content, or at least content that differs from theirs.

Maybe you are creating the content from a different perspective that will make it more interesting to the reader, or maybe you are using a different format to engage the niche. Maybe you introduce videos, where currently only written articles exist.

This is a big-picture first step. Try to get a good feel for what's out there, so you can top it.

2. Visit industry forums to pinpoint industry problems/topics of interest.

Looking at competitors' content is a good place to start, but you need to deliver the best content possible. How do you determine what the best possible content is?

You ask your niche.

In today's information age, there are online forums for everything. Find online forums where people in your niche interact, and join them. Read and comment on the forum threads, and ask probing questions to understand the biggest challenges people in your niche face.

This can be a time-consuming task, but one well worth every minute spent. If you can identify three to ten problems or challenges, you can then create dozens (maybe even hundreds) of pieces of content around them.

This is exactly what I did with my book *Engineer Your Own Success,* and eventually The Engineering Career Coach website. As an engineer myself, it was easy to identify a list of career challenges engineers struggle with. They included goal setting, effective communication, finding a mentor, networking and building relationships, organization, obtaining the right credentials, and leadership.

Naturally, these are the seven points covered in my book *Engineer Your Own Success.* They are also the fundamental topics that my partner and I have used to write hundreds of articles, and create over 150 podcast episodes (downloaded over 1,500,000 times) on The Engineering Career Coach website.

In the case studies section at the end of this chapter, I will discuss how I came up with The Content Marketing Equation and used it to create an entire book worth of content (which you are now reading!), based on discussions with content marketers and business owners.

You don't need a lot of topics to create great content, but you do need the ones that matter. By going directly to your readers through online forums, you can obtain the information you need to be the best in your industry.

The Content Marketing Equation

3. Look at books in your niche.

Another great way to come up with content creation topics is to look at books in your niche.

While you do not need to read all of these books, I do recommend reading at least a few niche-specific titles. For this exercise, all you have to do is go to a website like Amazon.com and type your niche into the book search engine. I might type 'engineering career development' when looking for topics to create content around on The Engineering Career Coach website and podcast.

You will likely see a number of books available in your niche. Select each book, click on the cover image, and you can usually preview the table of contents.

Skim through the table of contents and you'll see that each of the chapter titles are potential ideas for topics.

Please don't skip this action item; it's too easy and too valuable.

4. Review agendas for industry conferences.

Another quick way to get topic ideas in your niche is to look at the topics being presented at industry conferences.

Again, this is not time consuming, as you don't have to attend the events. Just do a Google search for events in your niche. I might try 'engineering career development conferences' for my site, The Engineering Career Coach. When you find some conferences, browse through the website and look for the conference schedule.

The schedule will list the topics being presented and

28

the speakers. This is a double win. Not only can you find topics that you can utilize for your website, but you can find experts on these topics. Now you can contact these experts and ask them to write a guest blog post for your site, or serve as a guest for an interview, which you then publish through any content channel you desire.

This is a great use of your time, as you can find several topics and experts in 30 to 60 minutes, without much effort.

5. Talk to people in your target market (online or in person).

I spoke earlier in this chapter about visiting online forums to get information directly from your target market. While this will definitely get you information that you can use to understand your market, there is nothing like talking to them in person.

Sitting down with people, or even just one person in your selected niche, can give you a wealth of information that wouldn't be as easily picked up through online forums. For example, a ten minute conversation with a young engineer could yield five to ten challenges he or she is dealing with, which could then be used to create five to ten articles or podcasts on The Engineering Career Coach website.

The best way to accomplish this is to attend a major conference in your market segment. This will give you the ability to talk directly to those who will ultimately consume your content. Fortunately, you already have a list of upcoming conferences in your niche from the prior section.

If you decide to attend a conference, make sure you are prepared with a good list of questions for those whom you speak with. Ask open-ended questions that cannot be answered with a simple 'yes' or 'no.' For example, "If you could change one thing about your current career situation, what might it be?" Another might be, "What is the biggest challenge you are facing in your career today?"

If you are on a strict budget and attending a conference is impractical, then you can still use online forums and talk to people over the phone. Use forums or social media sites like LinkedIn to connect with people in your target market, and explain to them that you are creating a resource for people in their industry and you would like five or ten minutes of their time for a quick phone call. You will be surprised by how many people will want to help you help them.

I have found that these one-on-one conversations spur amazing creative ideas for content development.

6. Purchase an email list and survey those on the list.

Another way to do market research is through surveys. However, the challenge with this method is that when you are starting out, you don't have a large enough email subscriber list to survey.

I will talk more about building your email subscriber list in the 'Capture' chapter later in the book, but there are some ways to gain access to your niche through email immediately. Namely, you could purchase an email list.

It's fairly easy to buy a targeted email list and send the subscribers a survey to quickly get information and data that you can use. But be aware, there are also several challenges that can come with using an email list you have purchased:

- You must find a reputable source to purchase the list from, and ensure that you have the rights, legally and ethically, to email that list.

- People tend to be angry when they receive an email from someone to whom they haven't given permission to email them. These emails will be seen by many of these people as spam, and will be flagged as such. This can hurt your email deliverability in the future, and they probably won't give you the information you were looking for after they mark you as spam. Lastly, this option can be very costly, and I have always tried to build my websites with little to no investment of my own money (or anyone else's, for that matter). Prices will vary depending on your industry and the size of the list.

So, while purchasing an email list may seem like a quick avenue to good information, this isn't always the case. I recommend trying to build your own email list using the rest of the strategies I will give you in this book. Or, reach out to a sponsorship partner, as I did with *The Stem Cell Podcast*. They may let you email their members, if it will help you deliver the best content possible.

All that being said, if time is of the essence, and you need information quickly, then consider purchasing a list after you have done your research. I recommend reading about the topic in Matt Paulson's book, *Email Marketing Demystified*.

7. Take a writing and/or copywriting course.

I've spent this entire chapter discussing how to collect data that will help you create content that is relevant and valuable to your target market.

However, you can have the best information available for your niche, but you still need to put that information into a format that will speak to your market.

In the next chapter, I will discuss creating and publishing your content across various channels; however, at this point I want to talk briefly about the importance of persuasive writing to content creation.

People's low level of engagement today is partly due to information overload. As a content creator, it is not good enough to simply write articles. Every post and every page on your website must grab your audience. Each piece of content must be written as a story, so the reader will want to follow it from beginning to end. Great content marketers are excellent storytellers, and at least decent copywriters.

I strongly recommend that during this process of gathering data about your market, you invest time and money into improving your writing skills as well. You should look into a general writing course, even if you took one in school, as well as a copywriting course.

This is another area where I could have done better. I became a better writer by writing a few hundred articles for engineers and a book, which I self-published. I paid for an editor on all of my early articles, which was very costly, at least $100 per month, which is a lot when you are on a budget. My book *Engineer Your Own Success*, was—from the standpoint of grammar and flow—mediocre. However, it was picked up by a major publisher who helped me greatly improve it. Their feedback made me realize how much I had to learn.

If you are on a budget, I recommend finding a low-cost writing course online where you have to submit writing assignments to keep yourself accountable. Also, take a course or read books on copywriting. I purchased and read all of the e-books on the CopyHackers website, which were absolutely invaluable to me.

Your ability to craft engaging and persuasive content is critical to the success of your brand.

8. CASE STUDY on Creating Valuable Content

Case Study #3 – This Book: *The Content Marketing Equation*

I am going to use the book you're reading as a case study for this chapter on creating valuable content. It's my book, so I can do that sort of thing. My niche for this book is: *business owners looking to use the Internet to grow their businesses.*

How did I craft this book's content in a way that I knew it would be interesting and helpful to this niche? I talked to many small business owners and helped them.

Because of the online portfolio I have built up, I regularly speak at conferences for entrepreneurs, and also receive messages asking me how I built up all of my different brands.

Rather than just telling people how I did it, I ask them questions about their specific situation. Doing this has helped me understand that a lot of these business owners do some things right, but aren't following every step in the equation.

Some of them published stellar content, but it was aimed at too wide of a niche, while others published below-average content to a well-defined niche.

Your experience in your niche, and your conversations with others, will drive the success of your content.

9. Your turn to take action on valuable content creation strategies.

Now it's your turn to take action and start creating valuable content.

Follow the exercises on the next few pages. I strongly recommend you don't start reading Chapter 3 until these exercises are complete.

INDUSTRY CONTENT

Review other websites in your industry, and write five to ten phrases that describe the content in the left column.

Your items might include: video is not used, articles are too long, and there are no good podcasts. In the right column, list five to ten things you could do to improve the content. Your items might include: start a podcast, utilize short videos, and write from the perspective of someone who has been successful in the field.

INDUSTRY FORUMS / CONFERENCES

Identify three industry forums or social media sites where you can engage with your audience (e.g., LinkedIn). Find five conference websites that you can look to for agenda items, and consider attending one.

_____

_____

_____

_____

_____

_____

CREATE A LIST OF TOPICS

Using the information in Sections 1 through 5 of this chapter, make a list of five to ten topics that you can create powerful content around for your niche. Be generous here: the more the better.

_____

_____

_____

_____

_____

_____

IMPROVE YOUR WRITING SKILLS

Perform an Internet search **right now** for either a course or a book on writing/copywriting and **purchase it**. Then schedule time on your calendar each week to improve your writing skills with the tools you have purchased.

Now you have a well-defined niche for your business, and a solid list of topics you can create content around. Next, I want to focus on employing multiple channels to get your valuable content into the hands of as many people as possible in your niche.

CHAPTER 3

Channels [C1] –
Publish Content through the
Right Channels

1. Creating your content across different channels.

If you have followed the first two chapters and completed the exercises at the end of each, you will have carefully selected a niche, and you will have a list of topics that you can now create content around.

In this chapter, you will learn how to effectively choose and utilize different channels to publish that content.

When I say channels, I am referring to both the format of the content (written articles, podcasts, videos, etc.) and the avenues through which you publish them (your blog, iTunes, YouTube, etc.). I will also give specific tips in this chapter on developing different pieces of content, namely articles, podcasts, and videos.

Before we dive in, let me reiterate the importance of quality writing in content development. Most content marketers start their content practice in a certain niche by blogging or writing articles. There isn't a rule that says you *must* start through written articles. You could just as easily build a brand through an audio podcast, or through YouTube videos.

But regardless of channel, you will find that writing is the cornerstone of all content development.

Whether I publish written articles, podcast episodes, or videos, I always start by writing an outline for each specific piece. I typically go through a handwritten brainstorming exercise, where I write down anything that comes to mind on a topic, and then organize those thoughts into one solid outline. Then, depending on the format of the content, I proceed in various ways.

For written articles, I will use the different sections in the outline as different headings in the article, and start writing each section.

For podcasts, I will jot a few bullet points beneath each section and then record my verbalized thoughts on each of the topics. I never write out a full script for podcast episodes or videos, just a detailed outline. In my experience, when I script an entire podcast episode or video, it comes out sounding completely unnatural, and I can't engage the audience as well as I do when speaking naturally and conversationally.

Once you have your list of topics and have created a few pieces of content, it will get easier. Because I have done it so many times, I am now at the point where I can create five valuable pieces of content in one day. If you follow the steps in this book, I am confident you will be generating high-quality content (and revenue) consistently.

2. Visit current industry content sites and gauge popularity of various channels.

At this point, you should have a pretty good handle on your competition, as you researched them when you were defining your niche in step one, as well as while determining good topics in step two.

Now, I want you to revisit the social media sites of your competitors. You should be able to clearly see which of their social media channels have the biggest following and, more importantly, the most engagement. This is important because many companies will buy Facebook fans or Twitter followers, but that doesn't mean those 'followers' are engaged or at all helpful to the success of their brand.

When I started The Engineering Career Coach Facebook page, we ended up using Facebook ads to grow our social following dramatically; however, the increase in fans didn't relate to any increase in engagement or sales. On the other hand, we have not done any paid Facebook ads for *The Italian American Podcast*, and—at the time of writing this book—we had less than 1,000 fans. Nevertheless, these fans were much more engaged than those on the Facebook page for the engineering podcast.

Here are some questions you can ask when visiting your competitor's social media sites:

- How many followers do they have on this channel?

- How active are those followers? Are there many comments and discussions going on through their channel?

- Are they doing a good job of posting on that channel? Depending on which channel you're investigating, a strong marketer should be posting about once a day (more for fast moving sites, like Twitter or LinkedIn's newsfeed), with 80 percent of posts referencing other people's content and 20 percent promoting their own.

- Are their social media sites easily accessible from their website?

Answering these questions for each of your competitors' social media sites should help you to determine which social channels are the best for your industry. You only want to spend time on those channels that will give you maximize return. Remember, your time is valuable; every second needs to be maximized.

I highly recommend that when you are doing your social media planning, you read some of Gary Vaynerchuk's material, especially his book, *Jab, Jab, Jab, Right Hook.* This book provides specific details on how to use social media effectively, as opposed to the general advice I have seen in many other social media books and courses.

3. Research the current trends in your niche.

Another quick and easy way to decide which channels to publish your content through is to see which format is most widely used in your niche. The best way to do that is to search online for the name of your niche and then the word 'news.'

By doing a quick search on 'Italian American News,' I can see the latest industry news and how it is being shared. Is it through written articles, videos, and/or podcasts? Are there social media channels that are coming up frequently in that search?

When I performed this specific search, a Twitter account for an Italian American news source was one of the top search results. This immediately told me that building a strong Twitter presence was going to be very important in engaging the Italian American niche.

Knowing the best channels to publish through is another quick and easy strategy that you can leverage in order to stand out in your niche.

4. Consider the 80/20 Principle (the Pareto Principle) in deciding on which channels to use.

In every business endeavor I am involved in, including building content sites, I rely heavily on the Pareto Principle—more widely known as the 80/20 Principle.

If you're unfamiliar with this idea, the Pareto Principle states that for many events, roughly 80 percent of the effects come from 20 percent of the causes. More simply, 80 percent of the results come from 20 percent of the efforts.

Management consultant Joseph M. Juran suggested the principle and named it after Italian economist Vilfredo Pareto, who—while at the University of Lausanne in 1896—published his first paper "Cours d'économie politique." Essentially, Pareto showed that approximately 80 percent of the land in Italy was owned by 20 percent of the population; Pareto developed the principle by observing that 20 percent of the peapods in his garden contained 80 percent of the peas. (Reference: https://en.wikipedia.org/wiki/Pareto_principle)

Think about this rule for a few minutes. It empirically demonstrates that 80 percent of the things you do are not effective, or do not contribute to your success. Building a business, or doing anything for that matter, without understanding and applying this rule can cause you to waste a lot of time, energy, and effort.

It is absolutely critical to apply this rule to your content marketing efforts, especially in deciding which channels to use to reach your audience. If you determine that your audience listens to podcasts regularly and don't consume a lot of video, then don't waste time there. If after one year in business, your Facebook page has generated zero sales, yet your Twitter account is landing new clients, focus less on Facebook and increase your use of Twitter.

This rule should not only be followed in starting or building your business, but I recommend utilizing it in every aspect of your personal and professional life. Your time is too valuable not to. If you are not good with finances or bookkeeping, pay someone else to do it. If one of your businesses is not profitable and one is extremely profitable, dump the one that is not and focus on the one that is. If you hate cleaning and are financially stable enough to hire someone once a week, make the investment.

In practicing the 80/20 Principle, you may just discover that you can build an entire brand and business by only creating videos and publishing them to YouTube. It's up to you to figure out what your 20 percent is, but the 80/20 Principle can be an amazing guide to help you find it.

If you want to learn more about this principle and how to effectively apply it, consider reading Richard Koch's books on the topic, or *The Four Hour Workweek* by Timothy Ferriss (which is something of a manifesto for online content business owners).

5. The art of blogging (written/audio/video).

You may think, or have heard, that blogging is a thing of the past. It's often remarked that blogging is old news.

This may be the case in your niche, but while I mentioned previously you should focus on the channels that will yield maximum results, blogging is still very important due to one word: Google. That's right, no matter how important video or audio is to your brand, search engines like Google still rely heavily on text.

No matter what media formats you use, written articles will always help people find you.

Blogging is not very difficult to do effectively once you have identified a niche and a list of interesting topics in that niche. Pick one of those topics, and either research it or lean on your existing experience/knowledge to produce a blog post. Here are the steps I follow when writing a blog post:

1. Decide on very specific topic for the article.

2. On a blank piece of paper or word processing document, brainstorm all of the important points within that topic.

3. Think of a catchy name for the article that encompasses the search keywords you are aiming for (see Section 5 in Chapter 4 for more about SEO).

4. Create an outline for the article based on the brainstorming exercise. I usually try to create different sections with their own headers for each point.

5. Write an introduction for the beginning of the post telling the reader what you plan to cover and/or what prompted this article.

6. Write the research, evidence, or argument beneath each section.

7. Finally, write a strong conclusion that includes a call to action for your audience.

8. Have someone proofread the post, add a nice photo or two, and publish it—using the keywords properly to maximize your SEO.

9. Share the post through your email list and social media sites.

There you have it. It's really not as hard as you think. If you are not a great writer, you can still go through the process and then have a good editor review and edit your posts. I promise you, if you write enough, you will get better and it will get easier.

Remember, the titles of your posts are critically important, especially for maximizing the traffic to your articles from your social media sites and email newsletters.

For example, I could write a blog post from this section of this book entitled: 9 Steps to Writing a Popular Blog Post; or, depending on the keywords I identify as important, it could also be titled, How to Write a Popular Blog Post in 9 Easy Steps.

You can also add video or audio to any of your blog posts to supplement your writing. This way, if your audience prefers video, they can simply watch the video. The text below the video will serve as 1) an alternate format for those interested in reading, but also 2) text for the search engines, to ensure you maximize your traffic.

I apologize, but you now no longer have an excuse NOT to write articles, no matter how poor a writer you think you are.

6. The power of podcasting (audio/video).

My major successes in content marketing have all come through podcasting. This is the channel that has allowed me to reach the most people and earn the most revenue.

Let me start by defining podcasting. A podcast is nothing more than a digital audio file (or series of files) made available on the Internet for download to a computer, mobile phone, or other portable media player. Should someone subscribe to a podcast, they are choosing to receive new episodes or installments automatically.

Essentially, a podcast is like a radio show on demand, as opposed to live. A huge benefit of podcasts is that they can be consumed 'on-the-go,' meaning anywhere—like during a commute to work, a workout at the gym, or even while doing yard work. You can now access your market at a time when the consumer previously couldn't engage with your written articles.

The four podcasts that I am involved with have been downloaded over 2 million times and have generated over $200,000 in sponsorships, over a period of approximately three years. Just as importantly, they have grown my brands, and helped to generate income in ways other than direct sponsorship—such as product and event sales. Podcasting is a very mobile content model, in that I can podcast from anywhere, and have even kept my podcasts going while spending 42 days traveling in Italy with my family.

I am not going to go through all of the technical details of starting or publishing a podcast in this book, but you can find a wonderful free guide online at www.PodcastingTutorial.com, which was created by Pat Flynn of Smart Passive Income. I used this tutorial when I launched each of my podcasts.

What follows are the crucial, can't-miss steps to publishing a high-quality podcast. To actually grow the show's following and scope, I recommend using all of the steps in this book. It should be obvious that the podcast you start will be in your niche, named for the niche, and that it will contain all of the valuable topics you have determined your market needs.

I also recommend being really smart about naming your podcast, and using similar strategies to those discussed for naming your business in Section 4 of the first chapter. As I've already mentioned, all my podcasts were the first of their kind, so I named them with a 'The' at the beginning, knowing that if I was out in front and had 'The' podcast in the industry, it would be hard for competitors to catch up to or replace my brands. Here are the four podcasts I am involved with, the first three of which I am a host on:

- *The Engineering Career Coach Podcast*
- *The Civil Engineering Podcast*
- *The Italian American Podcast*
- *The Stem Cell Podcast*

Assuming you now have a name for your podcast, and you have the initial setup complete, the following are the steps I follow for each podcast episode I publish. You'll notice that the steps are somewhat similar to those I follow for blogging.

Decide on a very specific topic for the episode. Make sure it's based on your research. I have found that the fewer topics it contains, the better an episode will be received. Also, by limiting the topics discussed on each episode, you will have content for several episodes. Decide if the episode will contain just you, or a guest interview. If the latter, reach out to said guest and set up the interview.

1. On a blank piece of paper or word processing document, brainstorm all of the important points within that topic. If you will be talking with a guest, ask the guest for their biographical information and some talking points that you can use.

2. Create an outline for the episode, based on your brainstorming exercise. I usually try to create different sections with their own headers for each point, or a bulleted list of the

points. The structure of your episodes may be driven by your listeners, which is important for listener engagement. For example, with my engineering podcasts, we make an effort to give the episodes very defined structure. One episode was titled 10 Steps to Obtaining Your Professional Engineering License. I'll let you guess what we covered. Engineers think analytically, so episodes with numbers and lists tend to be better received. This is another benefit of really understanding your niche; you will know how to best engage them.

3. Based on your outline, create a script for the episode. For each of the podcasts I am associated with, our teams have created a standard podcast script, which we customize for each episode. For example, the show might start with, "This is the Italian American Podcast, the first podcast dedicated to, etc." The script also outlines the different segments, and includes any sponsorship advertisements that have to be read. As I mentioned earlier, I don't script out my episodes word for word. I have tried doing this, but it comes off too mechanical and sounds like I am reading—because I am. Instead, I just list the main ideas in bullet points and then talk freely about each point while recording.

4. Review your script and then record the episode. I won't go into the details of recording an episode, as you can find that information online, but I do use Skype with a call recorder called Ecamm for episodes that contain either

a co-host and/or an interviewee. If it is just me, I record in GarageBand on my Macbook Air. I also use a Roland portable recorder when I am traveling, or recording episodes on project and event sites.

5. Perform the audio editing. This is a big step. While most recording programs will give you a fairly decent sounding result, you want your podcast to sound professional. I made the decision early on that I **would not** do the audio production or editing on any of my podcasts, and I have stuck to this. It is not my specialty and it would not be a good use of the 20% of my time I should be focusing on, based on Pareto's Principle. I found an audio producer using the freelance website Upwork, and he has been with me ever since, across all of my podcasts. He charges about $15 per hour, and typically it will take him anywhere from two to four hours per episode, depending on the length. This is another example of putting the Pareto Principle into practice and spending your time on the 20% of tasks that will generate 80% of results.

6. Write up detailed show notes for the episode. Show notes are nothing more than a summary of the episode that listeners can refer to or read through. The way I publish my podcast episodes is to create show notes, which are essentially a blog post on a WordPress website. I then insert the media file URL, which is hosted on a third party website called Libsyn, and publish the episode through my blog (this

is all covered in PodcastingTutorial.com). Once it is published on my blog, the podcast episode automatically publishes it to the major outlets that I have set up, like iTunes, Stictcher, iHeart Radio, etc.

7. Think of a catchy name for the episode that encompasses the search keywords you are aiming to target. Ensure these terms are located throughout your show notes.

8. Have someone proofread your post, add a nice photo or two, then publish it, making sure you use the keywords properly to maximize your SEO. (I'll talk more about SEO and making your content visually attractive in Sections 5 and 6 of Chapter 4.)

9. Share the episode through your email list and social media sites.

If you do all this correctly, you will be accessing two of the biggest search engines in the world, Google and iTunes. That's right—iTunes is a search engine, a big one, that people tend to forget about. In my opinion, this is why podcasting gives you such a huge advantage over content marketers who only blog. I had been blogging for years through The Engineering Career Coach site, but it was only when I launched my podcast that the brand really started to gain traction.

The other huge advantage of a podcast is that if your listeners subscribe through a podcast player, every time you publish an episode it gets pushed to their devices automatically. In some cases, it will even pop up a notification that a new episode is live. A podcast allows you to get your message and content into the eyes and ears of your target market quickly and efficiently.

You can also add video to your podcast for a third dimension, but this will require more time and work. I have also found that guests being interviewed tend to prefer audio only, but again, if your niche demands video, then add video.

There you have it. This is the strategy I have used and continue to use to create high-quality, engaging podcasts episodes that have been downloaded over two million times. That's my recipe distilled, for your use.

7. Video Marketing 101.

Video is another powerful channel through which you can publish high-quality content for your niche. I hadn't done too much video content until recently, when I started shooting and producing videos for the non-profit engineering organization I work for. We have had tremendous success, which I will discuss in the case studies section at the end of this chapter.

For now, let me go over the basics of video marketing, should you wish to incorporate it into your content development. If you plan to use video as your primary content channel, you should consider consulting with a video expert and/or studying the latest technical video trends and tips. I will reference some experts at the end of this section who may be helpful.

The benefit of videos is that they can garner very high engagement. In today's world, it is much easier to get someone to watch a video than to have them read through an article, especially a lengthy article.

I am not going to go into lengthy details on video, because I am not an expert, but here are a few things I've learned through experience:

The shorter the video, the better. Now, there is absolutely a time and a place for longer videos. One of those times may be if you are selling a high-priced product, or you are explaining a very detailed process. However, in all of my experiences, I have found that shorter videos win, every time. Even if you have a long, detailed process you are explaining, split it into a series. You can even host them all on the same page of your website, but split the videos up into one to three minutes each so they can be easily digested.

1. Lighting is critical to video quality. I have done some research on this. You can shoot amazing quality videos with an iPhone, as long as you have good lighting. You can purchase inexpensive lights on Amazon.com that will greatly increase your video quality.

2. Wear a light-colored shirt. My research and experience has taught me that wearing lighter colors, with minimal patterns, provides the best image for video.

3. Minimize background distractions. Try to keep a blank background or something plain like a wall with one photo on it. This helps to keep the focus solely on you and your message.

4. Prepare a script. If you are new to video and/or public speaking, I recommend writing out the script and using a teleprompter. You can purchase inexpensive teleprompters on Amazon.com. If you are comfortable speaking, then consider just writing out a list of bullets and speaking freely on each one for a more natural look.

5. State the video's benefits up front. I like to start my videos with, "In this video I am going to give you three simple strategies to achieve XYZ." This grabs the attention of the person watching, and also gives them an idea of the length and endpoint of the video. I can't stand watching a video that provides me with no idea of when it will end or what information I am going to receive.

6. End with a call to action. As with all good pieces of content, you should end with a call to action. Whether it be to sign up for your email list, purchase a product with a discount cou-pon, or simply subscribe to your video channel, you must call your followers to action, or they will never take the final step.

7. Keep the video editing to a minimum. By shooting short, well-thought-out videos, you can avoid having to pay a video expert to

produce and finalize them. I do all of my movies myself through iMovie. I can get a video finished in an hour at this point, although—like I said—I am not an expert and don't do it too often.

8. I recommend publishing your videos to YouTube, which of course is owned by Google, and making sure to write a detailed description for the video to get some SEO traction. YouTube is the second largest search engine on the internet. I also recommend writing an associated post on your WordPress website with the video embedded, to get maximum exposure through both Google and YouTube. Plus, on your site you can engage your audience directly, and benefit from the traffic through ad revenue or by capturing their email addresses and then selling them products or services.

These are some video tips based on my experience. I will share more on the power of video through a specific example in the case study section at the end of this chapter.

In the meantime, Caleb Wojcik has a good Do It Yourself video course at DIYVideoGuide.com, which also offers a more robust paid course. Or a simple Google search can bring up a huge amount of video production information.

8. Leveraging the right social media channels.

It's helpful to think of your content outlets as channels. Social media sites are also channels, which can be used to share both your content and that made by others.

If you have followed the steps in this book up to this point, you have already performed the research and figured out which social media channels are best for you to use.

The following are some items I have found to be helpful in maximizing my social media return. I am not a social media expert: I have learned these on my own while building my content websites. I think it is important for me to mention that I am not an expert in social media, because you need to know that you don't have to be. My expertise lies in creating the content and building the brand. I have put social media to good use, and you can deploy it effectively by keeping the following tips in mind:

- Pick the right social media sites to utilize. I will continue to say this over and over, because not doing so is the most common mistake. You don't have to be using all the social media sites, only the ones where the people in your niche live.

- Craft a powerful profile description and use a high-quality photo that represents you and/or your brand for each social media site you utilize. Photos of a person will always achieve more engagement than a faceless logo.

- Think of social media as a way to become a thought leader in your niche. Post your content, but also post other content that will help people in your niche. If they click on an article that you shared and they get value out of it, they will attribute the value partially to you, whether or not you created it, because you *gave* it to them.

- As a general rule, post information from others 80 percent of the time and your content 20 percent of the time.

- Use images to grab attention in your social media posts.

- Use short links, like Bitly.com, to track which social media sites are giving you the most traction.

- Post consistently. This is important. I can't tell you how many times to post on a social platform, because each one is different. If you go too long on a platform without posting, your site will look stagnant. When I investigate the social media presence of a company, I always look at the last time they posted. If it was weeks ago, it tells me they are not very active social media users.

When I go to conferences and meet people for the first time, they often say to me, "Oh yes, I follow you on LinkedIn. The information you share is very helpful." That's how you establish thought leadership. People recognize you as a major source of information in your niche, and social media is a perfect avenue to help you achieve this leadership status.

9. Take risks and be unconventional (my story).

Now it is time for me to contradict myself. Up to this point, I have preached doing your research and finding out the best channels to use, while establishing where people in your target market spend most of their time.

This all makes sense, but it is good to take a risk every so often and do something totally different. Be unconventional. Be the first to do something new in your niche.

I started my first podcast, *The Engineering Career Coach*, about three years ago. I vividly remember sitting in my hotel room in Anchorage, Alaska, in the midst of a 10-day speaking tour with my book *Engineer Your Own Success*, and hitting the publish button on Episode 1.

I had been preparing to launch the podcast for about four months, and during those months, all I heard was negative advice from people. One piece of advice I specifically remember was, "Engineers will never listen to a podcast about their career development." I think it is safe to say, one million downloads later, that they were wrong.

I took a risk. I spent time, energy, and money on building the podcast, and this channel changed everything for The Engineering Career Coach company. It allowed us to reach thousands more engineers through iTunes, and the podcast has generated six figures in sponsorships, as well as converting products and service sales.

The podcast is still the leading podcast in the niche of engineering career development, and continues to grow every day. So don't be afraid to go off the beaten path, every once in a while. Just make sure that if you do, you weigh the risk versus the reward to ensure you don't spend too much time on an endeavor that won't yield a high return.

10. CASE STUDIES on Publishing through the Right Channels

I want to give you two very specific case studies on publishing through the right channels, specifically through LinkedIn and video marketing. You can see a list of all of the case studies in this book in the table of contents.

Case Study #4 – Using LinkedIn Groups Effectively

LinkedIn has a section of the site known as Groups. It is a very powerful aspect of LinkedIn, because it allows you to join groups with thousands of members in a category or industry. What's even more powerful is that these groups are very specific. For example, I am a member of several civil engineering-related groups that have over 200,000 members.

One of the components of these groups is the ability to start a discussion on any topic, which everyone in the group can see and comment on. For years now, I have used these discussions to share the content I produce for professionals in that niche. I share the content through my status on LinkedIn, and then in just one more click, I can deliver it to as many of my groups as I want through the site's discussion feature.

This has been powerful in several ways. First, I get feedback on my content through people in the group commenting on the posts. This feedback is invaluable. Secondly, the content is immediately exposed to many people in the niche. Further, LinkedIn sends out regular group digests, which many of the members receive by email. My discussion is often listed at the top of the email. This is huge.

I still use this strategy today; however, LinkedIn Groups have become inundated with people using the same strategies. In order to stand out, you need to make sure your content is stellar, you have captivating titles for your discussions, and you engage the users through your post.

One way to engage users is to frame the discussion as a question: "I had the opportunity to interview Jim Smith on BIM modeling—have you used BIM modeling on your civil engineering projects? Do you agree with Jim's advice on the topic?"

This strategy has been crucial to the growth of The Engineering Career Coach company, including both of our podcasts.

Case Study #5 – The New York State Society of Professional Engineers Video Marketing

I have the honor of serving as the Executive Director for The New York State Society of Professional Engineers (NYSSPE). NYSSPE is a wonderful non-profit organization that serves to defend and promote the lawful and ethical practice of engineering and to ensure the safety and health of the public in New York State.

One of the biggest challenges with growing the NYSPPE membership is the fact that NYSSPE spends time, energy, and money on lobbying and legislative work that benefits all licensed engineers in New York (over 20,000), whether they are paying members or not. This legislative work often deals with issues that are extremely important to the success of engineers and engineering companies. The challenge is making engineers aware of what our lobbying work actually consists of, how it helps them, and why they should become paying members to support it.

We recently decided to turn to videos to accomplish this. So far, the response has been remarkable. We retain a lawyer who does the lobbying on our behalf. He does brilliant work, much of which goes unnoticed by our members and prospective members. I decided to invite him to the office regularly, record conversations with him about his work on our behalf, and use them to create a series of NYSSPE Legislative Video Updates. The videos are simple two to three-minute pieces that we shoot with a Canon camera, which I edit myself in iMovie. We email out a new video every two weeks.

We have received more positive comments and feed-back on these videos in the past few months than we have in the previous three years that I held this position. What's even more important is that engineers are start-ing to understand the importance of what we are doing at NYSSPE, and they are more excited to support us.

Since we started, people have made comments to the effect of, "NYSSPE has really gotten their legislative act together lately." We have been doing the same legislative work for almost one hundred years, but we just never used the right channels to explain it to people.

11. Your turn to take action on content channel planning.

Now it's your turn to take action and decide which channels to publish your content through.

Complete the following exercises. To make real progress you must take real action.

YOUR CHANNEL PLAN

Based on the information from Chapter 3, perform a brainstorming exercise and list all of the possible content channels that you could utilize to share the valuable content you create. Hold nothing back in this exercise. Use a blank piece of paper and list all possibilities and opportunities. Some examples might be a podcast, a very specific video series, a Facebook group, Instagram, Snapchat, etc.

Once you have completed the brainstorming activity, go through all of your ideas and select the ones that you believe will produce the best results (remembering the 80/20 principle). Talk to other people in your niche, including your audience, competitors, or peers, about which channels they have had success with.

On the lines below, write down the channels that you plan to start publishing through. If you plan to start with one or two channels and expand to more in the future, then simply write "future" next to the ones that won't be created immediately.

_____

_____

_____

_____

_____

CHAPTER 4

Consistency [C2] –
Publish Content Consistently

1. Establish a content schedule.

Publishing content consistently is one of the most important aspects of building a content brand, if not *the* most important aspect.

You've probably heard it said, "Content is king," but I think the saying should be, "Consistent content is king."

You will never be able to build up any type of reputation or following in an industry if you post randomly, whenever you get a chance. If that's your strategy, stop reading this book now, and save yourself hours of work that will yield little to no results.

Seth Godin writes one of the most popular marketing blogs in the world. He writes a post—even if it is short—just about every day. I subscribe to his blog and I look forward to the emails I receive with his new posts.

The Tropical MBA Podcast is a popular podcast on the topic of building location-independent businesses. The podcast is excellent and the information they provide is top notch; it's one of the reasons I am writing this book in the midst of a 42-day trip through Italy with my family. However, as good as the information is, there is one particularly important aspect to this podcast. At the end of each show, one of the hosts says, "We will see you next Thursday at 8 a.m. Eastern Standard Time."

The first time I heard the host say that, I thought to myself, next Thursday at 8 a.m.? This is a podcast. It's not live. You listen to a podcast whenever you want to listen to it. It is on demand. Isn't it? But over time, I realized what the hosts were doing. They were building consistency and credibility with their listeners. Because the content in this podcast is valuable as well as dependable, I now find myself specifically looking for their new episode every Thursday morning. Brilliant.

The best way to ensure that you publish content

consistently is to create a content schedule. This doesn't have to be an elaborate document. We use a simple, shared Google spreadsheet in each of my content businesses, so that the entire team can see and modify the schedule as need be.

The schedule should contain the following items:

- A row for each piece of content that you plan to publish, including blog articles, podcast episodes, videos, etc.

- A column for the publication date of each item.

- Another column for the date the content will be prepared. As an example, for podcast episodes, we set the date of the interview for that episode. This is helpful on occasions when we need to shuffle the schedule around, as we always know how far we can slide something. If we conduct an interview in August for an October episode, we can slide the publication date of that episode to September if something else falls through.

- A column that lists the topic. This allows you to ensure you are continually changing up the topics in the future.

These are the basic items that I highly recommend. Some other items that we use on our content schedules include:

- A column indicating if the content has been submitted to our audio producer (for our podcasts). This allows our content manager to ensure the episodes are on schedule.

- The name of the person who is being interviewed for each content piece (if applicable).
- Rows at the bottom of the spreadsheet where we list potential guests.

Please don't try to build a content business without a content schedule. This is the number one way to ensure that your content is published consistently and that your brand consistently grows.

2. Create a process for each channel.

If you are planning to grow a sizeable content-based business, it is very important that you create a process or a standard operating procedure (SOP) for each channel that you plan to use. This will not only ensure that your content maintains quality as you scale, but it will also allow you to easily delegate certain aspects of the content development process if they are no longer serving your 80/20 approach.

Contrary to popular belief, you can delegate many components of content development. Maybe not the actual writing or podcasting (although you *can* get help with that), but many of the other steps between the idea for a content piece and its publication can be delegated.

For most of my content businesses, we use a shared notebook in Evernote for all of our SOPs. We have a very specific SOP for the publication of a blog post that lists all of the steps involved, and indicates who is responsible for each step. Just to give you an idea, here is a sample of how the blog post SOP might look:

1. Determine topic for blog post.

2. Author to draft blog post in a Google Document.

3. Author to share the draft blog post with another Author for review and editing.

4. Upon completion of review, article is submitted to the Content Manager for importing to the website.

5. The proper SEO steps are performed on the article (see Chapter 4, Section 5 for more details on this).

6. A photo is added.

7. The post is tagged properly.

8. Author then does a final review and publishes the post.

9. The team then shares the post through social media.

This is just a quick sample, and not the entire document, but it is representative of how we build our SOPs. It looks pretty straightforward, and in many ways obvious, but you might be surprised how easy it is to miss a step when you aren't following a process. We also have a separate SOP for articles that are written by guest authors, which includes e-mail templates for reaching out to them.

Having good processes in place will also allow you to introduce automation into your business wherever possible. Automation is when things happen automatically (get it?!) without you having to do something. For example, when we book a guest on The Engineering Career Coach podcast, the guest fills out a form with their biography and talking points as part of our process, and then he or she gets redirected to a calendar where they can book an appointment. I am not even involved in that part of the process, yet the appointment just shows up on my calendar. I will talk more about automation in the chapter on monetization.

Your SOPs will become the backbone of your content business. They will eliminate redundancy between team members, save you time, and—most importantly—allow you to delegate steps in the process, which will be critical to your ability to scale your content business beyond yourself.

3. Set aside content creation days.

As you may have already figured out, I am very strategic when it comes to developing and publishing content. By strategic, I mean I put a lot of thought and effort into planning and preparing before I actually create the content. As I mentioned earlier, I prepare outlines and scripts before the actual writing or recording is performed, and work from a schedule that includes all content to be published.

To make the most of all your content preparation, you must set aside specific times of the week to create the content. You need windows of time to actually write your articles, record your podcast episodes, and shoot your videos. DO NOT just wing it and plan to create content whenever you have free time. You never will.

If you are building a content business, then content is your business. You must treat it that way and allocate time for development. I prefer the very early morning for writing (5 a.m. to 7 a.m.) and later in the morning for podcast recording (10 a.m. to noon). The early morning writing sessions allow me to write while it is quiet and generally distraction free. Over time, you will figure out what works best for you.

4. Don't miss a publication date.

If you want to build a content-driven business, it is extremely important that you publish content when you say you are going to, whether you say it publicly or just have an internal content schedule.

You must have the discipline to stick to your content schedule no matter what challenges arise. You will always be able to find excuses not to publish. I can't tell you how many times the sound quality of one of my podcast episodes was too low to publish, so instead of missing an episode, I sketched out a valuable episode on paper and recorded it. Missing a publication date shouldn't be an option.

You have to pledge to yourself, and to your audience, that you are going to publish on a regular basis, whether it is three times a week or two times per month. In the case studies section at the end of this chapter, I will talk about a huge challenge one of our podcasts faced, and how we overcame it and continued producing content consistently.

Please reserve content development time and be strict in adhering to it. It will pay off big-time.

5. Hire help for non-creative tasks as soon as possible.

When I started my first content business, I did everything. I mean everything. I had no staff and no money to pay anyone. I had to do it all. Once the business started to grow, I immediately started to outsource tasks that didn't explicitly need to be done by me.

I started small and hired a virtual assistant through the website Upwork (which was oDesk at the time), but as the business grew, I ended up promoting the same virtual assistant to a full-time role.

The process that I used to help me delegate effectively was simple. One day I realized that I couldn't scale the business on my own, so I sat down with a large sketch pad (24 inches by 36 inches). On one large piece of paper, I wrote down every single task that I did, and broke them down by frequency (daily, weekly, monthly, etc.). Then I went through all of the tasks and highlighted the ones that didn't necessarily have to be completed by me. I was shocked to see that more than half of them were highlighted.

From that day on, I had at least one or more virtual staff to help me with the tasks that could be delegated. I am not suggesting delegation for the sake of delegating. You delegate when you no longer can keep up with your content production schedule on your own and/or you want to focus on more business-building activities. At this point in time, I try to only do two things: 1) the actual content development, and 2) sponsor outreach to earn revenue, which I will discuss later in the book.

Some tasks that staff can help with include research for your content development, maintaining your content schedule, researching and reaching out to prospective guests, coordinating with guests for interviews and guest-written articles, graphics development for your content, and preparing show notes along with graphics for podcast episodes.

As you grow your business, you will get better and better at deciding what to do yourself and what to delegate.

Delegation is critical to the growth of your business—always remember that.

6. Include SEO in your process, but don't compromise readability.

I defined and spoke briefly about search engine optimization (SEO) in Chapter 1 Section 4, but in this section I will go into more detail on how you can do your own SEO without paying an expert way too much money.

SEO is critically important to any content-based business. No matter how valuable your content is, if people can't find it, it really doesn't matter. Since I am not an SEO expert, I use three primary strategies for SEO success with my content.

First, I learned the fundamentals of SEO. A friend referred me to the book *Search Engine Optimization: An*

Hour a Day by Gradiva Couzin and Jennifer Grappone. This book is a guide to SEO for business owners who want to learn about the topic and spend a little time each day improving the SEO on their website. I highly recommend reading this book, or a more current book on the fundamentals of SEO, as the SEO rules change on a very regular basis.

Secondly, I do a search for frequently-searched keyword phrases that cover topics of interest in my target market, but don't have a lot of competition online. I don't necessarily look for the phrases that get searched 1,000 times a day, because those phrases are already on so many websites that I will never rank on page one of Google by using them.

I look instead for the phrases that get about 75 to 100 searches per day, but have very little competition, so I know that by using them, I can rank on page one of Google, and high up on page one at that. The reason for this is simple—who ever clicks through to page two on Google?

There are different programs that you can use to search for these phrases. If you read a current book on SEO, you will be able to determine some good programs or websites that source the best phrases. I used a program called Market Samurai, which cost me about $100, but was extremely valuable. I will discuss some of the success that I had in the case studies section at the end of this chapter.

Lastly, I use a WordPress plugin called SEO by Yoast. When activated, this plugin appears on the back end of every page and post on your website, and essentially scores the SEO for the keyword you have selected on that page, with suggestions on how to improve it. Some of the steps that it will recommend for you include:

- Ensure the keyword phrase is in the post title and URL,
- Place the keywords in the first paragraph of the post,
- Utilize the keyword phrase multiple times during the post (the total number will be dependent on the total post length),
- Use two photos in the post that are tagged with the keyword phrase,
- Utilize heading text that includes the phrase.

That's it. Those are the only three steps that I have used on my sites to build up some good SEO traction. One other item that is helpful is getting links to your website from other websites. The idea here is that if a reputable website in your niche is referring to your site, then search engines will give you added credibility and be more likely to refer your site. I honestly didn't spend much time on this one; however, due to the value I provide, people started posting about it on their websites without me asking them to. If you create quality content and publish it consistently, the backlinks will come.

Don't make SEO harder than it is. Follow these steps and your site will be in better SEO shape than most content websites.

7. Make your content visually attractive.

If you are building a content website, you will be fighting other content websites for the attention of your readers. Thousands of other articles may stand between you and a prospective reader, so you need to ensure that your content is attractive to the eye.

As mentioned earlier, the title line will certainly play a role in attracting readers, but so will graphics. I learned this the hard way, by not using graphics early on. When I finally figured out how attractive good photos and artwork can make your content, I made it a standard part of our content development process. Graphics will also help your SEO, as detailed in the last section.

There are many royalty-free stock photo websites out there that you can use; however, here are some tips that I can offer on visual attractiveness based on my experience. While your experience may be slightly different, I am confident that some of these tips will be useful in improving the visibility of your content:

- Place full width photos in your post, as opposed to a portion of the width with text on the side. Personally, I feel it is terribly distracting to try to read text with a photo embedded next to it. I typically place photos at the top of our posts to set the mood.

- If you plan to use stock photos, I recommend using scenic vistas or photos with symbols in them as opposed to a group of people dressed in suits. If you want people in the photo, use a photo of yourself or another photo that you have taken, as it will look more authentic.

- This may be obvious, but make sure you have permission to use or else purchase the rights for all photos you utilize on your website, and reference them properly.

- Consider photos that will really grab the attention of prospective readers when your content is posted on social media.

- If you are interviewing someone for a podcast episode, ask him or her for a nice photo of themselves. This will be much better than a stock photo.

Photos give your content another dimension. Take advantage of them, and make them as authentic as possible. While there are many free stock photo websites online, I recently started using Adobe Stock, which isn't free but has more attractive photos that have really improved the visual attractiveness of my websites.

8. Consistency is where you can win BIG with content.

I've spent this entire chapter giving you strategies to help you achieve consistency with your content production, and there's a good reason for that. In a world of too much content, consistency is what will separate you from your competitors. I have found that publishing content consistently is an extremely difficult thing for people and businesses. It requires a lot of focus, dedication, and hard work.

This is why I love producing content. If you are willing to focus, work hard, and follow the steps in this book, you can be a thought leader in your niche. I can't tell you how many other content creators in the engineering space told me they were going to start a podcast. Most of them did, and I tried to help them grow by promoting them. However, after a few episodes, they stopped. They couldn't keep up.

I recommend that if you are planning to grow a content business, create your content schedule and commit to one year of production. Don't just plan the first month or two, because once you get through a year, you are much more likely to continue to publish consistently.

Consistency is your secret weapon—your silver bullet. Not many people can do it, but if you can, you will be rewarded for it.

9. CASE STUDIES on Publishing Content Consistently

I want to share two case studies on the topics in this chapter, one on SEO, and one on how we continued to publish content when *The Stem Cell Podcast* lost both its hosts.

Case Study #6 – SEO on Top Engineering Company Posts

When I was building The Engineering Career Coach brand, I was thinking of ways to increase the website traffic. The challenge was growing it in a way that would attract engineers in our target market.

I decided to use an SEO program that I mentioned earlier, Market Samurai, and I found a group of keywords related to 'top engineering companies.' I proceeded to write a series of five posts on the topic that—since publication—have yielded over 400,000 visits to our website.

I figured that engineers who are looking to work at top firms are engineers who are looking to advance their careers. The SEO program that I used told me these terms were heavily searched, but that there weren't too many websites using them, which allowed me to rank high on page one on Google.

These posts have hugely helped our brand by providing a major source of email opt-ins, boosting traffic which helps gain sponsorships, and also increasing our Google AdSense revenue.

Here are the names of the posts:

1. The Five Larger Best Civil Engineering Firms to Work For

2. Top Electrical Engineering Firms to Work For

3. The Best Engineering Consulting Firms to Work For

4. Five Larger Top Structural Engineering Firms to Work For

5. How to Start an Engineering Company: Owning and Managing an Engineering Business Through a Tough Economy

I am not an SEO expert, but the couple of minutes that I spent on this keyword search and the few weeks spent preparing these articles have had a major impact on the success of our website.

Case Study #7 – A Podcast with No Hosts

A few years ago my brother, who is a stem cell scientist, decided that he wanted to start a podcast on stem cells. So he asked a colleague to co-host with him, and he asked me to be a business partner and handle the online marketing aspect of the business. *The Stem Cell Podcast* was born.

The podcast, which is still going today, provides stem cell scientists with summaries of the latest industry research papers, and delivers interviews with top-notch scientists in the field.

Utilizing the equation in this book, my partners and I built the podcast up tremendously, collecting over six figures in sponsorship income within one year. Then it all came crashing down. For professional reasons, both my partners had to step down from hosting the show.

We found ourselves in a very difficult situation. We had an extremely popular brand, with paying sponsors, but no hosts. After many phone calls and text messages, we came up with a plan to continue the show.

We immediately started looking for and interviewing prospective hosts. We explained the situation to our sponsors and told them that we were going to take a break from the audio podcast for roughly two months while we brought on the new hosts. However, during those two months, we continued to publish the research paper summaries and guest interviews in written form, with links to the sponsors' websites.

We ended up finding two amazing hosts, and we stuck to our two-month re-launch schedule date. We kept on two of the three sponsors, and our first few episodes back were downloaded more times than any of our previous episodes. The show is still ranked in the Top 100 science podcasts on iTunes at the time of writing this book.

Dealing with this situation was probably the biggest and most stressful challenge that I have dealt with in any of my content businesses, but my closest partner insisted that we stay calm and keep trying through all of it—and we pulled it off. Which was important, since he's also my brother.

The most valuable takeaway was that we were essentially able to swap out the hosts of an extremely popular podcast, and still continue to grow the brand. To me, that makes me feel better about all my content businesses; it proves they are not 100% host/creator dependent. This also gives us a case study that we can use if a sponsor says, "What if something happens to one of the hosts?"

10. Your turn to take action on publishing content consistently.

I am going to go easy on you in this take action section. All I am going to ask you to do for now is to establish a rough content schedule for the next year.

Maybe it doesn't *sound* that easy, but let me help you get started. In the table in this section, or on a blank piece of paper, mark out two columns and twelve rows. In the first box, write the name of the month you plan to start publishing content, then fill in the rows below with the names of the next eleven months.

In the box beside each month, write a topic/theme for the content you plan to publish in that month. If you are trying to figure out how it's possible to plan so far ahead, try using the times of the year to your advantage. For example, you can write on topics related to the holidays during November and December. In January you can potentially focus on goal-setting, if that makes sense in your niche.

I still go through this process of planning topics for the upcoming year at the end of every calendar year, because it is that important to keeping all my businesses publishing content consistently.

DO NOT TURN THE PAGE until you have at least two topics listed in each box.

Month	Topics
January	
February	
March	
April	
May	
June	
July	
August	
September	
October	
November	
December	

CHAPTER 5

Capture [C3] –
Capture Information

1. Capture email addresses from day one on your website.

At this point, if you have followed the steps in this book, you will have: determined your niche, started to create valuable content on relevant topics, identified the right channels to promote yourself, and planned to publish that content consistently. If that's the case, you either have, or will soon have, people in your target market visiting your website.

This chapter covers the last component of The Content Marketing Equation, which is capturing the information of those individuals that visit your website.

Imagine doing all of the work that I have described up to this point in the book, right up to getting targeted traffic to your website, but then not capturing the information of those prospective customers. It happens more often than you think. In fact, in my experience, it's the biggest mistake small business owners make.

You must—and I repeat you must—attempt to capture the email addresses of the visitors to your website from day one.

There are so many low cost tools available today to help you collect information. We use the Thrive plugin on our WordPress websites to create a popup box that is connected to our email programs, which right now is either ConvertKit or MailChimp depending on the business.

In order to capture the email addresses of your website visitors, you'll need to offer something valuable in return. What you give them in return is called a lead magnet. In this chapter, I will cover the entire email capture process, from lead magnets to autoresponders, so you don't make the same mistake that most business owners make.

After reading this chapter and implementing the steps, you will be able to immediately start collecting information, segmenting, and engaging with a high percentage of your website's visitors.

2. Lead magnets matter.

The first step in collecting an email address from one of your website visitors is to offer that person something of value in return. I need to emphasize the word VALUE with respect to lead magnets.

How many websites have you seen where there is a shoddy looking sign-up form in the sidebar that says, "Sign up for our newsletter." When I see that, the first question I ask myself is, "Why?" For what reason should I sign up for your newsletter?

If you plan to use your newsletter as a lead magnet, you *must* make the offer sound much more attractive than, "Sign up for our newsletter." This is where the copywriting skills I referenced in Chapter 2 Section 7 come into play. Here are a few sample pitches to entice visitors to sign up for a newsletter:

- Sign up for our newsletter for insider tips on building your online business.

- Sign up for our newsletter, and we'll send you three business-building tips that helped us increase our revenue by 20%.

- Sign up for our newsletter and join the thousands of entrepreneurs who are getting access to our insider business building tips (*please only use this metric if it is true—you can always change it to hundreds*).

- Sign up for our newsletter, which is focused on helping business owners save time, and increase revenue.

These are just a few examples, but hopefully you get the point. If I am going to give you my email address, I had better be getting something good in return. I need something that is valuable to me. Just adding one sentence like this to your sign-up box can have a huge impact on your conversion rate, and ultimately your revenue—if your revenue is related to your email list.

I have had a lot of success across my different businesses in building email lists, and there is no doubt, the quality of the lead magnet is directly proportional to the conversion rate.

Here are some tips based on my experience of collecting more than 10,000 email addresses. That number may or may not sound like a lot to you, but remember, I focus on very narrow niches:

- The more relevant your lead magnet will be to a visitor, the higher probability that he or she will opt-in. For example, if someone lands on The Engineering Career Coach website through an article on how to prepare a resume, it's safe to say this person is looking for a new job. If we have a lead magnet on the end of that post offering a resume template, the conversion rate will be higher than if we just offer access to our newsletter. In the case studies section of this chapter, I will walk you through the segmented opt-in process we use on The Engineering Career Coach website.

- Experiment with different lead magnets regularly on your website until you find the one(s) that convert(s) the most. I have found that, contrary to popular belief, longer or more substantial lead magnets aren't necessarily more successful than simple ones. I've seen people have just as much success with a simple one-page PDF as other people have with an elaborate video series or e-book. Don't make assumptions, as every niche is different. Test, test, test.

- Your lead magnet must contain information that will improve the life or career of the person signing up for it. The benefits must be clear. We are all busy today, and we only have time for things that matter. Catering to this mentality when you design your lead magnet will greatly increase your opt-in rate.

- Survey your niche through your mailing list, or through an online forum/social media site, to try to determine their biggest pain point. Then design a lead magnet to alleviate that pain.

- Promise instant results with your lead magnet, and deliver. We are in a world of immediacy. Today matters and no one cares about tomorrow.

These tips should help you plan for powerful lead magnets that can directly drive the success of your content-based business. In the next section, I will give you a more detailed example of the development of a lead magnet to make it make it easier for you to develop your own.

3. Deciding on and creating an opt-in lead magnet.

In the last section, I talked about the importance of a good lead magnet and how it can dramatically increase your email subscriber opt-in rate. I gave some general examples based on my own experience, but in this section, I'll walk you through the details of one of my own successful lead magnets from beginning to end, to give you a blueprint to follow. Here is the example, along with some general steps to follow:

- **Research** – Firstly, do research to try to determine the biggest challenge that your audience is facing. I will use our podcast *The Stem Cell Podcast* as an example. We determined through talking with stem cell scientists that it took them a lot of time to keep up with trending research. To do so, they would have to read the newest research papers soon after they were published, on top of their already busy research schedule. So we identified this as a big pain point that we could help remedy.

- **Solve** – Next, brainstorm different ways that you could help your audience solve their problem. In the case of a lead magnet, you want to help them solve their problems, in exchange for their email addresses. As mentioned earlier, potential lead magnets could include writing an e-book on the subject, an audio file, a simple PDF, or even a series of pre-written emails delivered over time. I have found that currently, easily digestible lead magnets are more desirable. For example, people would rather scan through a one page PDF, then sign up for a 20-day free email course. Back to our example: we thought that we could solve stem cell scientists' research paper problem by providing audio summaries of the most recent papers on *The Stem Cell Podcast*. This was a huge hit, and it was one of the reasons the podcast grew as quickly as it did. Not only did we summarize the research papers on the audio podcast, we provided written summaries in the podcast show notes (also known as episode summaries) on our website.

- **Develop** – Next, package your solution into one of the content examples I have suggested, or another one that fits your audience. This step may include shooting a few videos in your office, writing a valuable e-book, or creating an mp3 file. In our case, we focused on crafting engaging paper summaries, both in the podcasts and in written form on our website.

- **Capture and Deliver** – This final step usually consists of creating the components needed to deliver the lead magnet to your subscribers and collect their email addresses. There are many different ways to do this, but the most common way is to upload the lead magnet to a landing page on your website, collect the subscriber's email address, and then immediately email them the link to the landing page that contains the lead magnet. A landing page is typically thought of as a page which only allows for one action by the visitor, which in this case is downloading or consuming the lead magnet. As I will discuss later in this chapter, you must be aggressive in collecting email addresses—consider using a pop-up opt-in form on your website. In our stem cell example, we added an aggressive pop-up box to our website that said, "The Stem Cell Podcast makes the lives of stem cell scientists easier by summarizing the latest research papers on the podcast. Enter your name and email below to receive new episodes as soon as they are published." This approach increased our email subscriber rate by 100% in the first few months.

I realize that creating a productive lead magnet can be time consuming, but when you are thinking with an 80/20 mindset, this is easily one of those 20% tasks that can generate 80% of the results in your business.

4. Segment your email list to achieve high engagement.

I've talked a lot about the 80/20 principle in this book, and here's another opportunity to apply it to your business.

Regardless of how well you follow The Content Marketing Equation, there will be people that visit your website and sign up for your email list who are not part of the niche you are servicing. This may sound harsh, but there is no reason for you to waste your time dealing with them.

People may sign up for your mailing list from a few different segments of your niche. When I say segments, I mean different disciplines in the same niche. For example, in engineering there are different types of engineering including civil, mechanical, electrical and chemical, to name a few. You could refer to these as segments. By segmenting your list, you will be able to send specific emails to each of these different types of subscribers.

There are two fairly simple ways to do this:

1. **Immediately offer a very specific lead magnet.**

   Let's say your niche is carpet-cleaning companies. When a prospect visits your website, you may have an offer that pops up that says, "Enter your name and email address, and we'll send you three tips that can immediately increase the revenue of your carpet-cleaning business." The box can contain three fields: First Name, email address, and a pull down box with four options: 1) We clean only residences 2) We clean only commercial properties, 3) We clean both residential and commercial properties, and 4) I am not associated with a carpet cleaning company at all.

2. **A second step segmentation.**

   Assume you make the same offer as outlined above, but your pop-up opt-in box only has the option for first name and email address. Then, once someone signs up, they receive an email that says, "Thank you for signing up to receive our tips to increase your carpet cleaning company's revenue. To ensure we send you information specific to your business, click the sentence below that best describes you: We clean only residences; We clean only commercial properties; We clean both residential and commercial properties; I am not associated with a carpet cleaning company at all."

In both cases, you are going to have an email list that is segmented in a way that will allow you to communicate with every person on your email list in a very customized and specific way. In my experience, option two is a much better option, as adding the pulldown option on the initial pop-up form has proven to drastically reduce the number of people that will sign up. I believe this is because people are busy and the more steps that you ask them to take, the less likely they are to take them. I will give a real example of segmentation from one of my businesses at the end of this chapter.

I highly recommend that you never ask for last names in your sign-up forms. The more fields you add to an opt-in, the more you decrease conversions. In fact, many people ask only for email addresses, not first names; but I recommend collecting first names, as it will allow you to personally engage with these prospects using auto-responders, which I will cover next.

The other huge benefit of segmentation is that you can avoid wasting time trying to service people who are not interested in what you are providing. Those who select the option, "I am not associated with a carpet cleaning company at all" will likely never buy from you. Make sure they get the lead magnet, but then remove them from your list or send them an automated email explaining that you primarily service carpet cleaning companies. Your email marketing program will most likely charge you per contact, so why pay for people that aren't prospective customers?

In addition to allowing you to engage in a more customized way and eliminate false prospects, segmentation allows you to customize your lead magnet, which greatly improves the user experience. In this example, you would create three different lead magnets. One geared towards residential carpet cleaners, one towards commercial cleaners, and one that ties both together. This is powerful.

Think about it. If you went to a sporting goods store to purchase a pair of sneakers, the sales associate might clarify your interest by asking, "What will you be using your sneakers for?"

If you respond, "I am a runner, and run a few miles every morning," then he or she will have narrowed down the options regarding which shoes they can sell you. You will also be more inclined to buy at that store, because you feel like you are getting shoes that are exactly what you need.

Gathering people's contact information and giving them the exact information that they need will separate you from many other companies in your niche, because unfortunately for consumers—but fortunately for you—most online businesses don't do this.

5. Engage through auto-responders.

People from your niche are visiting your website, and you are not only collecting their information, but you are segmenting them into very specific lists. What do you do now?

You engage with them!

I know what you may be thinking. I am not planning on collecting just a few email addresses, or even a few hundred. I am thinking bigger, so how can I effectively engage with each of the thousands of people that come through my website? Once the segmentation is set up, you will have a few different lists in your email database, and you can use auto-responders to communicate with them.

Auto-responders are nothing more than a series of emails that are automatically sent out to a person once he or she opts in to a certain list. If you collected the first name as I recommended, these emails can be personalized as well, giving readers a much more individualized experience of your brand.

Consider the carpet-cleaning example I gave earlier. If a residential carpet cleaner signed up for your mailing list, they may get an email right after the segmentation email that says:

Hello Anthony,

We know your business is focused on residential carpet cleaning, and we know at times it can be difficult to maintain and grow revenue in this industry. However, we have experience helping residential carpet cleaners become financially successful. As promised, here is your list of three tips that can help to immediately increase your business's bottom line.

Enjoy the information, and I will check in with you in a few days to see if it was helpful.

Anthony Fasano

Carpet Cleaners Central

Author of Carpet Cleaning Book

Notice that this email is very specific to their business. It is also short and to the point. It mentions the value that the lead magnet will deliver, and lets the person know you will follow up with them, which opens the door for the second email in your auto-responder series. This follow up may be an inquiry, where you ask them if they had any questions on the information you sent. Notice that the signature line cements my credibility in the field by listing my book on a topic relevant to the niche.

All of my businesses have auto-responders in place, some more elaborate than others. These auto-responders allow you to build a relationship with every prospect that opts in to your email list, without having to manually write each of them. Then, at some point in your auto-responder series—once you have built up your prospect's trust by delivering value—you can start to sell them on your products and services. After all, that is the name of the game in business: **revenue**. We will discuss monetization more in the next chapter.

Most email marketing platforms offer auto-responders. In my experience, Convertkit offers the most robust but simple auto-responder function; however, the paid version of MailChimp also has pretty good auto-responder capabilities.

6. Be ten times more aggressive than you feel comfortable with in asking people for their information.

This is another mistake that I made in building my first email list with The Engineering Career Coach website. I wasn't aggressive enough when asking for people's contact information.

Until I met Matt Paulson, who wrote the Foreword for this book, I was vehemently opposed to using what is known as a pop-up box on my websites. A pop-up box, also known as an opt-in box or opt-in form, typically pops up within the first few minutes of someone visiting your website, asking for their information in return for your lead magnet.

I always felt that these were terribly intrusive and annoying, and many people had indicated that I should avoid using them. But in my conversation with Matt, he explained to me how his company, MarketBeat, had successfully used pop-up boxes to collect hundreds of thousands of email addresses. You read that correctly—hundreds of thousands.

He also mentioned that you could adjust pop-up boxes so they weren't as intrusive; meaning you can set them so they only appear when you scroll down, and—once your reader clicks out of the box—it won't come back for a set period of time (like 30 days).

After that conversation, I implemented pop-up boxes

across all my content websites, and that move has changed everything. For example, on The Engineering Career Coach site, we went from approximately two opt-ins a day to 11. Think about what kind of an impact this can have on your business, especially if you sell a product or service. It's monumental.

No matter how uncomfortable it makes you feel, be ten times more aggressive than you would like to be when collecting people's information. This strategy may be the difference between your online business succeeding or not.

I still read all of Matt Paulson's content on business building. You can find all of his books at MattPaulson.com, including his book on email marketing, entitled *Email Marketing Demystified*, which covers many of the topics discussed here in more detail.

7. Collect email addresses at conferences and speaking engagements.

We get so wrapped up in the world of online marketing and opt-in boxes that we can sometimes forget that there can be tremendous offline opportunities for building an email list.

I spent about three years traveling around the United States, from Maine to Alaska, with my book, *Engineer Your Own Success*. I gave over 40 talks to thousands of engineers, but there was one thing I did during those speaking engagements that is still paying off to this day. I collected email addresses.

When I decided to become an executive coach for engineers, I knew I was going to have to speak often to get my message out. So I took a course entitled, *How to Become a Six Figure Speaker* by a woman named Kathleen Gage. I still have the binder with all of the course work. During the course she recommended giving out a survey at the end of every speaking engagement to 1) gather data from your market, and 2) obtain email addresses.

If you give a talk to a group of people, and the information in the talk is valuable, they are very prone in that moment to want more of your information. Though I was able to sell some books after my talks, it was more important that I gathered people's contact information while they were primed to give it to me.

All I did was add a line on my survey that said, "I send out periodic emails to engineers with similar information from my presentation tonight. If you are interested in receiving them, please clearly write your email address here." That one course I took, and that one line on a survey, helped me to gather thousands of very targeted email addresses. I can't tell you how many seminars I go to where the speakers don't ask for any feedback or contact information.

While at conferences, you can also collect email addresses if you have an exhibitor booth. If you take this route I recommend three specific strategies:

1. Have a valuable offer if you plan to ask someone for their contact information. For example, raffle off something either expensive (that they

wouldn't get otherwise) or extremely specific to their needs.

2. While talking to people, make notes on the back of their cards about which ones are good prospects. (Everyone wants a new flatscreen television; not everyone wants to receive your emails. But they'll give you a business card either way.)

3. Follow up with the good prospects after the event.

Most people who do this simply load all the email addresses they collect into a database, and then send out a blast email selling something. I don't recommend one blast to all of the email addresses you collect, unless there is such a large number that you can't follow up individually. Remember what I talked about earlier in this chapter: the more specific you can be with people, the more inclined they are to buy from you. If you kept clear notes on each prospect, attempt to follow up with each of them individually, as warranted. Worst-case scenario, just add them to your newsletter list, and they will get future correspondence. Again, there's no need to hit them all with a one time, "thank you for visiting me at the conference" email.

Take advantage of offline opportunities to gather email addresses when they arise, as most people don't.

8. Your email list is your business, period.

Content creation is a great way to build a brand, but it only works if you utilize the content to capture information from your website's visitors; most importantly, their email addresses.

Yes, you can also build up a large social media following, but there is still nothing as direct as email. Every so often I hear people say, "Email is dead." Not true, at least not currently, in 2016.

Email is a direct communication line with people, and your content can help you build up an email list for your target market. It doesn't always matter how big your list is; what matters is who is on it. If it is filled with people in your niche, who are interested in your products and services, then you will have the ability to scale a sizeable business.

Without the ability to monetize that content through an email list, you may be creating stellar content, but you probably won't be able to sustain it forever.

9. CASE STUDY on Capturing Information
Case Study #8 – The Engineering Career Coach
Lead Magnet and Autoresponder Setup

As I mentioned earlier, it took too long for us to start aggressively collecting email addresses on The Engineering Career Coach website, but we now have a very effective process. In this case study, I will walk you through our process so you can see all of the details, and hopefully apply some of them to your business.

If you were to do a Google search on something related to engineering career development, there is a high probability that you will land on The Engineering Career Coach. The reason for this is that, in building the site, we followed the five steps presented in this book as The Content Marketing Equation.

When you land on the website and scroll down just a little, an opt-in form pops up asking you if you would like a free three-part video series created just for engineers. The box specifically says:

3 Keys to Engineering Career Success

FREE videos that will yield immediate results

- *Short, easily-digestible videos*
- *Tips for maximizing LinkedIn with examples*
- *Proven techniques for quicker promotions*

If interested, you put your name and email into the sign-up form. Immediately, you are sent an email that asks you to select the option that bests describes yourself. The options provided include:

1. *I am an engineering student, but not a civil engineering student.*

2. *I am a civil engineering student.*

3. *I am a recent graduate engineer (non-civil engineer) with 0 to 5 years experience.*

4. *I am a civil engineering recent graduate with 0 to 5 years experience.*

5. *I am a young engineer (non-civil engineer) with 5 to 15 years experience.*

6. *I am a young civil engineer with 5 to 15 years experience.*

7. *I am an experienced engineer (non-civil engineer) with more than 15 years experience.*

8. *I am an experienced civil engineer with more than 15 years experience.*

9. *I am not an engineer.*

This may seem like too many options, but it tells us a lot about you, and then we can communicate with you in a very specific and customized way. Remember, we segment civil engineers because we have a podcast for civil engineers, and have found that a large number of the site visitors are specifically civil engineers.

Once you select your focus and experience level, you immediately receive the first video, and of course, the video is specific to your experience level. So we actually created 12 different videos for these sequences, to make sure that each of the four different experience levels receive very individualized information.

From this point, the videos will be delivered to you over about ten days. After that, the autoresponder continues to send you relevant information and also attempts to sell you products and services that make sense for your current experience level. You will also receive our weekly newsletter with our most recently published content.

We are currently averaging 11 sign-ups per day, which equates to over 4,000 email addresses per year. We use a program called Convertkit as our email software, which makes it easy to implement complicated autoresponder sequences.

The linchpin in our entire strategy is that the information we capture is specific. We know how many engineers are in each experience bracket, and we can communicate with them in an individualized way. This makes the user experience much better, and also makes it easy for us to sell very targeted products and services to them, which increases sales conversions.

I will talk more about revenue in Chapter 6—Monetization.

10. Your turn to take action on capturing contact information.

Now that I have laid out the processes that work for us in capturing information, it's your turn to design a process for your business, that will work based on your niche.

First, I want you to come up with three different possible lead magnets that you can use to convince people in your target market to give you their email addresses. It could be a written article, video, audio, or even a simple PDF with a checklist.

Come up with three really good ones and then you can narrow them down, or possibly test a few different ones. You must be sure that the lead magnet is extremely valuable to the prospect and that you will be able to convey that value in a few simple sentences. Please jot down five ideas now:

_____

_____

_____

_____

_____

Now based on the lead magnets you have come up with, I want you to try to come up with different possible segments for those that might opt-in. Do you want to segment your list by experience level, income level, business size, or other categories? It is really important to communicate with your prospects in a very specific manner. Please make a list below of possible segments.

Completing this exercise now will ensure your success tomorrow.

_____

_____

_____

_____

_____

Once you have completed these exercises, take your list of possible lead magnets to some trusted colleagues and advisors for their opinions, then select the one you want to develop first, and determine a schedule for implementation. Make this project a priority.

Remember, your email list *is* your business.

CHAPTER 6

Monetization –
The Scary M Word

1. Think big picture monetization strategy.

So far, I have spelled out The Content Marketing Equation for you. This equation will help you to build your content-based brand into one of the strongest in your niche. You will be publishing superior content for a very specific niche and capturing contact information of people consuming your content.

Now, how do you get paid for your content?

This is the question all content creators ask at some point in the building of their business. You publish free content and build a following, but in order to turn it into a real business, you have to generate revenue. I did not include monetization in my actual equation because most of the businesses that focus on making money from their content produce horrible content. You must focus on executing the equation first, and *then* monetizing it.

In Chapter 1 Section 7, when deciding on your niche, you considered all potential revenue sources in your field. Now it is time to act on that initial plan and make any adjustments needed, based on your newly acquired experience publishing content in the niche.

I recommend starting with a reasonable revenue goal that you would like to achieve in the next 12 to 18 months. For example, let's say you set a goal of $100,000 in revenue in the 18 months from today. Next, you must come up with a plan breaking down the different sources for that $100,000. Your plan may look something like this:

- $85,000 – content sponsorships
- $10,000 – products and services
- $5,000 – website income

Content sponsorships would include companies that pay you for an advertisement on your website, podcast, or any other media channels that you publish through.

Products and services would depend on your niche, but would essentially be a way for you to earn money from those consuming your content. Products and services could include paid-for webinars, one-on-one or group coaching, books, online community membership, and more. There are a lot of different options for products and services, you just have to design them based on the needs of your niche. I will give you some examples of products and services I have utilized in the case studies section at the end of this chapter.

Website income may include avenues like Google AdSense, which allows you to insert ads into your content. With Google AdSense, every time a visitor clicks on an ad, you earn income. There are other companies and offerings like this; you just have to decide how many ads you really want to have in your content.

If you are just starting to monetize your content business, I recommend that you focus mostly on sponsorships. They will most likely be the biggest source of income, and they don't take up a ton of time. In fact, I would pour 80 percent of your efforts (outside of content creation) into sponsor outreach.

If you took the time to find a well-defined niche, there are likely companies looking to put their brand in front of your niche market. This is what happened with the stem cell podcast, which was able to generate over six figures in sponsorship income in one year. I will discuss this process in detail later in the chapter.

When it comes to monetization, don't let the 'M' word scare you. Come up with a plan and execute it. If you have built your content using The Content Marketing Equation, monetization will be easier than you think.

2. Passive versus active income.

Before we get deeper into monetization, I want to talk about passive versus active income. Most people think they can decide to build an online business, and then—just by flipping a switch—they will earn large amounts of passive income.

This just isn't the case.

Building an online business requires a lot of work, and very few online businesses have a *truly* passive income model.

Let me define passive and active income for those of you new to online businesses and marketing.

Passive income is income that is earned regularly because of something that requires minimal effort to maintain, which was done previously. A product is one of the most common forms of passive income. One of the best examples of this, in my opinion, is a book. It takes a lot of hard work, but once you publish it and list it on Amazon, you simply collect royalties when it sells. Obviously the more you market the book, the more it will sell, but the income earned from sales is passive.

Another good example of passive income comes from my own experience. A company who sells online courses to engineers and engineering companies asked me to record three courses in their studio a year ago, and now, I get a check every month for royalties from every sale. This requires *no* maintenance on my end. Currently, it is going so well, I may ask them if we can produce more.

On the other hand, active income is income for which ongoing services have been performed. If you provide coaching services to a client, and in return they pay you, that income is active income. Active income can be very lucrative, but you have to constantly work for it. Plus, if you stop, the money stops coming.

I recommend that early on in your business you earn whatever income you can, but—for the long term—focus on building passive income. I consider content sponsorships active income because, if you stop producing content, you can't obtain sponsorships.

That being said, you are reading this book because you are building, or want to build, a content-based business. If that's the case, sponsorships offer an excellent source of income. Even though it is technically active income, with sponsorships you typically don't have to get bogged down dealing with a lot of people. And if you plan to create the content anyway, why not get paid for it?

In this chapter I'll discuss different ways to earn both active and passive income, but please think truly passive income for the long term. I will give you some examples at the end of this chapter to help you monetize your business.

There are many exaggerated online business stories about securing huge amounts of passive income—these are often false. Don't worry about what other people have done; focus on your own monetization plan.

3. Solve problems through products and services.

As described in the previous section, products and services can serve as vehicles to monetize your stellar content. Regardless of whether you are looking to build active or passive income, your audience must need your products and services, and they must be high quality. Otherwise, you will be wasting a lot of time creating them.

I have found that the best products and services solve a problem. Problem-solving products and services sell much better than those that look to improve a situation or make lives easier. The best phrase to summarize this idea is, "Your products and services must be painkillers, not vitamins."

Figure out what products and services to develop by surveying your readers and listeners. You can do this through social media, but the most valuable responses will come from a survey that is emailed out to your mailing list. These are the people that you will be pitching the products and services to once they are ready for sale, so their input is critical.

Keep your survey simple. No more than five questions. Ask multiple-choice questions like, 'What is your biggest challenge right now?' Come up with four answers, but then also give them the opportunity to enter in their own. You may also want to ask how much money they are willing to spend to solve their biggest problem. Give ranges so you can get an idea for pricing.

Many content marketers think just because they have

a lot of readers or podcast listeners, they can simply package their content into a bundle and sell it for a lot of money. Not true.

To be clear, your content *can* be re-packaged into a product like a book, which in essence makes your content the product. However, if you can find out which topics garner the most interest, then you can create products that will sell to more people. You must create painkillers for your followers at the right price point, and your research should tell you exactly how to do that.

4. Know your volume requirements for income generation.

In Section 1 of this chapter, I talked about looking at your big picture plan for monetization. Once you have done that and performed some research to determine the challenges in your niche, you will have a good idea of what painkilling products and services you should create.

Now, before you start production, you need to get even more detailed. Based on the data you have collected, consider how many products and/or services you *must* sell in order for it to be worth your time in creating them.

Start with the number of people that responded to your painkiller survey. Let's say 100 people responded, and 75 of them experienced the same challenge. Of those 75, assume 50 of them said they would pay $200 for a product that would solve their problem. Of those 50, estimate that half would actually purchase your product or service. That would equal $5,000.

If you are an experienced online business owner, you may be saying, "There is no way you are going to sell to 50% of your list during a product launch." I realize this sounds aggressive, and potentially unrealistically inflated; however I have seen this happen many times when the business contains segmented email lists as discussed in Chapter 5. The segmented lists serve to pre-qualify those subscribers, ensuring you are sending them information that interests them, which in most cases improves conversion rates.

How does that fit into your big picture monetization plan? Does it make sense to move forward with that product or service? Do you need to build up more of a following first? Can you find others who have mailing lists in your niche, who you can sell through by paying an affiliate commission?

My point in this section is very simple. Developing products and services requires time, energy, and (in some cases) money. You don't want to invest your time, energy, or money unless you have some very good data that suggests your products or services will sell. Trust me, I have developed several courses that sold very little, and looking back, it was a terrible use of my resources.

Later in the chapter, I will give you one more step that will guarantee you don't waste your time, energy, or money.

5. Don't wait too long.

Regardless of what income vehicle you decide to utilize for monetization (sponsors, products and services, or website income) don't wait too long to attempt to monetize your content brand, unless you are doing it for the pure joy of creating content.

Good content takes time to develop; therefore, if you are going to spend your time developing it, you want to make sure that it will generate revenue at some point in the near future. Otherwise, you will be on the content hamster wheel for a long time.

You'll recall that the content hamster wheel occurs when you are creating free content over and over for your subscribers. They love it, but aren't paying for it, and you just keep on producing without stopping to figure out how you will ever be able to make a living off of it.

I have been there too many times. Only recently did I establish my new rule: I no longer develop content for free. My content always has to generate revenue in some way.

In fact, I have changed my business model, and I now do more paid-for content development. If a company or association is looking for content for their members or subscribers, they will pay me to create it. In order to succeed in a business like this, you need to set time limitations.

There is no doubt that growing a content business and a following takes time, but you don't want to spend years on the content hamster wheel. Use some of the strategies I have discussed in this chapter to gauge how quickly you can start earning revenue with your content. Use these same strategies to figure out how much revenue you can make.

6. Seek sponsors but don't compromise your content.

As much as creating products and services for your subscribers can pay off, I still think the fastest and easiest way to monetize content is through sponsors, affiliate agreements, and advertisers. They have a lot of money, and if you follow the steps in this book, you will create (or have created) a platform of prospective customers for many companies in your niche.

Many people cringe at the word sponsor. They think that putting sponsors or advertisements into their content will ruin it, and all of their subscribers will run away. This doesn't have to be the case. If your content is good enough, your content consumers will barely notice the ads.

If Starbucks put advertisements on their cups or on their app, would you stop buying their coffee? No you wouldn't, because you need it, and you love it.

You may be leaving thousands, or hundreds of thousands, of dollars on the table if you decide you want to keep your content sponsor-free.

Here's another perspective to consider that might make you feel more comfortable seeking sponsorships. What if you found a sponsor that has a product or service that would greatly help your subscribers? What if they gave your subscribers a discount through their advertisements? In this situation, everyone wins.

Your fans get access to a needed product or service, at a discount. Your sponsor gains visibility and acquires some new customers. Of course, you also earn revenue. This is the perfect trilogy. This is called a win-win-win relationship, and you need to look for these as soon as possible in your business.

Another key strategy is asking listeners (or other parts of your audience) to support the sponsors, because the sponsors help to keep the content free.

By saying this, you're stating a simple fact.

Unless you plan to run on the content hamster wheel forever with no money to show for it, your sponsors allow you to keep producing the content that is helping those in your niche. Your listeners should understand that, and you will be surprised by how interested they will be in supporting you and your sponsors.

In the case studies section at the end of this chapter, I will talk about how I was able to generate over $200,000 in sponsorships of my my podcasts, in a short period of time.

All of that being said, you want to make sure that if you do seek and acquire content sponsors, you don't sacrifice the quality of your content in the process. Let me repeat that. **Do not sacrifice the quality of your content in any way to obtain a sponsor.**

This is where sponsorships can pose problems for content marketers. I've had situations where sponsors wanted to have their employees repeatedly interviewed on one of my podcasts as part of the package. Ultimately we agreed, but the language of the agreement made it clear that we had to approve the final content for the interview. The language also indicated that the content had to be of value to our listeners, otherwise we would have the opportunity to exclude it from the episode.

We are actually going through this now with one of our company's podcasts. We are having problems obtaining sponsors, because most of them want their staff interviewed on the show, but we don't believe that this approach will be of interest to our listeners. This is a problem that takes some tact and diplomacy to navigate properly.

The best approach here is to explain to the prospective sponsors that force-feeding their products and services to your subscribers isn't likely to yield a lot of sales. Instead, taking the positive approach of letting your subscribers know that this brand is helping to keep the content free, and asking them to support your sponsor, is a much better approach for all parties involved. Win-win-win.

I highly recommend that you look for sponsors that can help your subscribers and develop the win-win-win relationships that I have discussed in this section. This is the fastest way to build solid revenue from a content-based business.

7. Automation equals income, as your time is valuable.

In Section 2 of Chapter 4, I talked about setting up processes for your content creation to allow you to introduce automation into your business. Automation is when things happen automatically, without you having to be involved.

Standard operating procedures (SOPs) and automation should also be utilized during monetization. The key to a good content business is to minimize the number of people you have to deal with outside of the content creation part of the business. Y,ou may want to interview people to enrich your content, but going beyond that will leave you open to unlimited numbers of people, who will eat up your valuable time.

In most of my sponsored content businesses, we have automated the correspondence with the sponsors as much as possible. This benefits both parties, and ensures the sponsors get the most out of our relationships. We use Google Documents to minimize the need for unnecessary correspondence.

For example, if we have a sponsor that changes up their message frequently based on the episode topics, we might build a Google spreadsheet specifically for that sponsor, which displays our upcoming schedule. The sponsor's representative can then look at the schedule at their convenience, create the company's advertising spots and banners, and email it to us in bulk.

We will also create a Google spreadsheet for our

sponsors where they can insert their spots for each episode. Then when it is time to prepare the episode script, we simply copy and paste the advertising spots from the spreadsheet into the show script. If the advertising spots are not in the Google spreadsheet two weeks before the episode, then—according to our contract—we simply use the same spots as the last episode. You don't want a sponsor's tardiness affecting your publication routine or schedule.

Your time is extremely valuable; it should be used primarily for content creation. Build processes and use automation wherever possible to ensure 80 percent of your time is spent in the right place.

8. Sell before you create if possible.

I've made it a point throughout this book to emphasize the importance of researching the needs of those in your niche. When you know what their challenges are, you can create content—and eventually products and services—to help them overcome those challenges.

I have learned the hard way that no matter how big a pain point you are trying to alleviate, you'll never know someone's willingness to pay for a product or service until you ask for their money. Doing a survey and asking for price ranges will certainly give you data, but getting someone to actually open their wallet is oftentimes much harder than you think.

That's why I am recommending here that you ask for

money *before* you spend time creating products or services. Fundraising platforms like Kickstarter have made this pre-sale process popular. I actually used a site similar to Kickstarter, called Indiegogo, to raise over $13,000 to write and publish two children's books with my daughter. We wrote the Purpee the Purple Dragon books, and delivered them to children with pediatric cancer all over the United States.

The basic idea here is to sell the product or service to people at a discount *before* you spend time creating the product or service, rather than spending the time to build out a product or a service which no one may want. This way, you'll know your time will not go to waste. That being said, with websites like Kickstarter, you don't actually get the money until it is funded. So keep that in mind when planning your project budget and schedule. Also, with fundraising sites like Kickstarter, if the project isn't funded, in most scenarios, all previous donations are returned and you end up with no money. This is another reason to be careful about your schedule and how much work you might have to do before you actually have the money.

I say a product or service because you can even pre-sell coaching services. Say you have an idea for a twelve-week group-coaching program helping entrepreneurs grow their businesses. In order to make this a premium service, you will need to build out a schedule for the group, which will include a curriculum of topics to discuss. You might also need to invest in software like GoToMeeting, which you can use to conduct the coaching calls.

Before doing any of that and going into development, why not sell the package to your subscribers at a discount? You can say that you are in the process of developing a new group-coaching curriculum for entrepreneurs that will launch in three months. You can offer spots in the group ahead of time, at a pre-sale discount of 25% off.

This allows you to see how many people will really pay for it, and ensures that you will hit your revenue goals. When someone purchases it in the pre-development phase, you let him or her know that if you don't get a certain number of people to sign up, the group will be postponed and they will receive a full refund.

Again it's a win-win, because they are getting a discount, and you are ensuring that you won't spend time and energy for little money.

This works even better with a product. You can use the same process, and offer a discount. You can also offer those that purchase the product in the pre-development (often called beta) phase the opportunity to offer input on the actual product. This is also a win-win, because it ensures that the customer's questions are answered, and it guarantees that your product is relevant. Plus, your pre-development customers feel invested in something they "helped" to build.

I spent months building a do-it-yourself, goal-setting course for engineers without pre-selling it. I ended up only selling nine copies of it, and did a lot of work that I was never reimbursed for. Since then, I have used the pre-development sales process.

You can even use this process with a content sponsor. For example, you could approach a potential sponsor for your new podcast and say, "I started a new podcast in the XYZ niche. We are only a few episodes in, but the early response has been great, and our research indicates rapid growth for the show. While our download numbers are still low, would you be interested in taking a six to 12-month sponsorship out at a very low rate. This will allow you to put your brand in front of prospective customers and grow with the podcast. Even though we are projecting massive growth for the podcast, you would lock in a low sponsorship rate for the next 12 months."

We took this approach with *The Italian American Podcast*. While we didn't profit from the agreement directly, it allowed us to avoid having to invest marketing money into the business at the early stages.

If you plan to build a successful content-based business, you will need to maximize every second of your time, which is why you can't spend time, energy, and money on building products and services, unless you know they will earn you money. It's a simple and in some ways obvious strategy that most entrepreneurs do not utilize—but now you can.

9. CASE STUDIES on Monetization

In this section, I want to talk about two of my content businesses, and how I was able to monetize them through sponsorships.

Case Study #9 – *The Stem Cell Podcast* Sponsorship Income

I mentioned earlier in the book that I am the co-owner of *The Stem Cell Podcast*, a niche podcast dedicated to providing stem cell scientists with up-to-date industry information to help them stay on top of their research. The show remains tremendously popular, even after we replaced both hosts, and is by far the leading podcast of its kind.

Because we followed the steps in The Content Marketing Equation, we were able to generate over $100,000 in sponsorship income over one 12-month period through this podcast. Here's the equation related to this business:

- **Niche** – we focused solely on stem cell scientists.

- **Value** – we provided valuable and timely content, because stem cell scientists have to keep up with the latest research trends.

- **Channels** – we published through channels that worked for stem cell scientists; we chose a podcast since scientists work in a laboratory and can listen.

- **Consistency** – we published consistently on every other Tuesday morning. Even when we were inbetween hosts, we published written summaries on those same days.

- **Capture information** – we use a pop-up form on the website to capture email addresses of stem cell scientists so that we have the ability to survey them for important information.

Because we followed this equation, and because there are several large corporations that sell tools and equipment to stem cell scientists, we lined ourselves up to earn the revenue mentioned earlier.

At any one time we easily had two to three companies who sponsored the show, and one time we had a headline sponsor that spent more than $65,000 a year on a multi-layered package. All because we followed the equation presented in this book.

Case Study #10 – The Engineering Career Coach Sponsorship Income

We followed the same equation with The Engineering Career Coach, and we were able to earn over $50,000 in sponsorships across our channels. The key was finding a company that led the way in selling exam preparation products and services to engineers for the professional engineer's licensing exam. They are essentially selling to the exact target audience that listens to our engineering podcasts.

This again is truly a win-win-win relationship. Most young engineers have to take and pass this exam in order to advance in their careers. We can now draw them to one of the best review courses available, and also give them access to a discount. On top of that, the sponsorship allows us to keep the podcasts free for those same engineers. Every party involved wins.

When you search for sponsors, look for sponsors who are serving the exact niche you serve first and look for the win-win-win relationships.

10. Your turn to take action on creating a monetization plan.

In this section, I want to help you put these monetization strategies to use for yourself, so you can avoid getting trapped in a content hamster wheel.

Don't get me wrong; there is typically an initial period with any good content business where you are working hard to put out stellar content, without earning income. That is the nature of content marketing; but with some forethought and planning, you can minimize the amount of time that your content business doesn't earn revenue.

Further, you might just build something that another entrepreneur sees value in, and is willing to pay you for. **I am currently in the process of selling one of my content businesses and, while it's too early in the process to give you the details in this book, it will definitely produce a financial return that was well worth my time.** Maybe that's a topic for another book.

Now it's time for you to plan your content monetization strategy.

Right now, based on Section 1 of this chapter, I want you to create your big-picture monetization plan. First, come up with the total revenue you would like your content business to generate one or two years from now, and then on the lines below list each revenue source, with their associated amounts. The example I gave earlier was $100,000 in 18 months, broken down as follows:

- $85,000 – content sponsorships
- $10,000 – products and services
- $5,000 – website income

_____

_____

_____

_____

_____

_____

_____

_____

Now I want you to create a more specific monetization plan for your largest potential source of revenue. Think of the 80/20 principle here. Write out a plan below for your largest potential source of income. If it is sponsorships, list prospective company names in your niche. If it is products or services, sketch out a schedule for the development of the product or service that you anticipate earning the most revenue.

I'll say it again: this is not just an exercise. It's a real step you can take to secure success in content marketing.

_____

_____

_____

_____

_____

_____

_____

Congratulations! You now have a more detailed monetization plan than most content marketers I know.

CHAPTER 7

Conclusion –
It's Time for You to Take Action

Building an online business is anything but easy. It takes a lot of hard work, done consistently over time. This book gives you an easy equation to follow, to ensure that you are doing all the work you need to grow your business online.

You have the ability, and now the steps needed, to leverage the power of the internet to build a revenue-generating business that can not only help people, but can give you a tremendously flexible, exciting, and enjoyable lifestyle.

I have three young kids, and I actually get to pick them up at school at 3 p.m. every day, do their homework with them, and coach their soccer teams, as opposed to getting home late from work and missing dinner with my family. In fact, my son just asked me last night, "Daddy why do you get up so early and work every morning?" My response was, "So I can pick you up every day from school at 3 p.m. and spend the afternoon with you and your sisters." Of course, he replied, "Well then, I like when you get up early and work."

But this book isn't meant to give you a rah-rah motivational story on why building a successful online business will be beneficial to your life. It's mean to inspire you to take ACTION, and build your business in a way that will get results.

There are no excuses from this point on. You have my proven equation, laid out in a very detailed manner. Now I want you to take the action steps at the end of each chapter that I have laid out (if you haven't already) including:

- Chapter 1 (N) – Brainstorm your **niche**.
- Chapter 2 (V) – Create a list of **valuable** topics for your niche based on market research.
- Chapter 3 (C1) – Decide on and publish your content through the right **channels**.
- Chapter 4 (C2) – Establish your content schedule for the next 12 months to ensure **consistent** content creation and publication.

- Chapter 5 (C3) – Design a process for your business that will allow you to **capture** the information of your content consumers.

There you have it folks, the notoriously complex world of online marketing and content creation boiled down for you into one simple equation: **NVC^3**.

I truly hope you can use this equation to create a business, and life, filled with abundance.

You can receive my latest content marketing strategies, and follow my latest content projects at www. EngineeredContent.com.

ABOUT THE AUTHOR

Anthony Fasano's expertise in content marketing was built through experience. Fasano has built several successful content brands and podcasts including *The Engineering Career Coach*, *The Stem Cell Podcast*, and most recently *The Italian American Podcast*. His Engineering Career Coach website was ranked the top career content site worldwide for engineers and his engineering podcasts have been downloaded over one million times.

Fasano has also co-authored a series of children's books with his 8-year-old daughter entitled *Purpee the Purple Dragon*. They have delivered hundreds of the books to pediatric cancer centers around the United States.

www.EngineeredContent.com